SALARY

4 profoundly impactful steps to
aligning your time and energy with
what feels joyous and fulfilling

Jessica Kaskov

For more information, email Jess@JoyfulnesswithJess.com

ISBN: 979-8-88759-641-9 - paperback
ISBN: 979-8-88759-642-6 - ebook
ISBN: 979-8-88759-643-3 - hardcover

Discover your
Soul Salary™ score

with this free assessment:

www.JessKaskov.com/SoulSalary

Are you a **High Earner** in Soul Salary, or are you **barely making minimum wage**?

<u>How it works:</u>
Answer twenty yes/no questions in under two minutes.
Generate results instantly.
Receive feedback to give yourself a raise in Soul Salary.

Dedication

To Riley and Parker - Remember to follow
your joy and that weird is a compliment.

Contents

Introduction..xiii

SOUL SALARY BASICS:

Chapter 1:   What Do You Do? 3
Chapter 2:   What is Your Soul Salary? 8
Chapter 3:   Demand Minimum Wage—It's the Law.........13

STEP 1: SOUL SALARY PAYCHECKS

Chapter 4:   Where is Your Joy? 27
Chapter 5:   What is Your Legacy? 37
Chapter 6:   Your Ideal ~~Job~~ Life 47

STEP 2: RAISES AND PROMOTIONS

Chapter 7:   Give Yourself a Raise! 55
Chapter 8:   Time for a Promotion....................................66

STEP 3: SOUL SALARY BILLS

Chapter 9:   Joy Killers 75
Chapter 10: Soul Suckers..82

STEP 4: BUDGETING AND BUDGET CUTS

Chapter 11: Toodles, Joy Killers 93
Chapter 12: So Long, Soul Suckers 105
Chapter 13: Budget Cuts 117

CONCLUSION

Chapter 14: Become a High Earner 127

Soul Salary Workbook.................................... 133-190
Acknowledgments 195
Want More? 197
Author Bio 199

A Pair of Glasses

It started with a pair of glasses
Rose-gold frames
Cat-eye shaped
They showcased my blue-green eyes
Highlighted my face
In a way my heavy dark brown tortoise shell frames didn't.

It started with a pair of glasses
I felt lighter, prettier
I started wearing bold colors and jewelry
to match my new-glasses vibe
I remembered self-care, self-love, self-trust.

It started with a pair of glasses
I searched my soul
I opened my heart
I allowed my joy to emerge

It started with a pair of glasses
Starting a chain of life changing events
From night school
To a new career
To writing a book.
It started with a pair of glasses
What will be your first step?

✦ ✦ ✦ ✦ ✦

Introduction

While I was picking out my glasses with my new prescription, I realized I was going through the motions of life. I had lost myself, but as the saying goes: "Sometimes you have to lose yourself to find yourself."

As I tried on pair after pair, I wondered to myself, *who am I?* I lovingly named some parts of myself as I processed. Am I Jessica, the industrial engineer for a Fortune 500 company, who makes lists in her sleep and loves processes? These practical, brown frames are perfect for Jessica. Or am I Jessileigh instead, the artistic, creative, spiritual, nurturing, rainbow-unicorn-inner-child? Wouldn't Jessileigh do better in these bright teal glasses?

I realized the answer was yes. I am both, and I am even more than that. I am all. I am Jess, and that includes all of my parts. I don't have to be one or the other. I can be all of me and all aspects of myself. And so, I chose the glasses I liked best, regardless of what I "should" have chosen . . . and I am so glad I did.

With this new insight—and new glasses—I embarked further on my self-discovery journey. This book includes stories on what I did for myself to find the true me, my true purpose. It will also offer advice so that you can start living with immense joy and fulfillment through the seasons of life.

I developed this concept of Soul Salary, which refers to the value your soul receives when your time and energy are spent in alignment with your passions, your life purpose and mission on Earth, and what feeds your soul. When I say soul, I want to honor whatever soul means to you, whether you think of soul as your essence or sense of self or add religious connotation to the word. In yoga, we often say, "namaste," at the end of the class, which means "that which is sacred within me salutes that which is sacred within you," and I want to include that intent here as well.

Soul Salary was meant to give another definition of salary besides the financial one we fixate on. I use this concept to develop what your soul considers paychecks (something that fills you up) and what your soul considers bills (something that drains you). For example, cuddling with my cat is a "paycheck" for my soul and cooking of any kind is a "bill." In other words, it is a way to be intentional on how you spend your time and energy. This book was written as I went through a profound Soul Salary journey and as I made big changes in my life. Many points in the book are in real time, notes and journal entries I did while I worked to bring more joy and fulfillment to myself. As many other writers before me have said in some variation, "Write the book you need," and I certainly did here.

This book takes you on a journey to discover what your current Soul Salary is today, to find your paychecks that fill you up, and to identify the bills that drain you. You will also learn about giving yourself raises and promotions, as well as doing some budgeting (and budget cuts!). The point is to keep doing these steps until you become a High Earner in terms of your Soul Salary. Once you do, your soul will feel warm, joyful, lit up, passionate, useful, happy, and fulfilled. Writing this book gave me what I needed to become a High Earner in Soul Salary, and I hope reading it does the same for you.

Throughout each chapter are exercises I have developed. They will help you keep all your reflections in one place to reference as you continue to work toward increasing your Soul Salary. Yes, I am suggesting you write in the book—even if your elementary school librarian would be mortified! This book is meant to inspire and be used for personal reflection. You have the answers. I am merely the guide to help you find them!

In my journey, I gave myself "raises" and "budget cuts" in Soul Salary. I became certified as a life coach, started studying writing/self-publishing, and eventually wrote my first book (this one!). I moved to working part-time in my corporate job. Eventually, I quit altogether, after over fifteen years in the supply-chain industry as an engineer and people leader, to pursue my passions of writing, speaking, and coaching full time. It was very scary to take the leap of faith into the unknown of entrepreneurship focused on spreading joy through my words. I jumped off the cliff with the intent of making my parachute as I fell. Nonetheless, I am so proud of the deep love, courage, and sense of worthiness it took for me to take each step.

Now, I am not saying that quitting your job is the answer for everyone, but creative possibilities are out there that can make your soul paychecks skyrocket and slash your soul bills. This book is about finding out how to be who you are wholly (building from the bottom up) to maximize your joy and fulfillment. By the end, you will have a plan for how to be unapologetically you and live your life on your terms—for your joy and for the legacy you want to leave. The moral of the story is to live for joy, live for you, live for your purpose, shed constraints, pressures, and expectations (unless they are your own grounded ones), and feel joyful and fulfilled. Journey into self-discovery, joy searching, legacy building, and shedding Joy Killers and Soul Suckers to allow in light, love, and happiness. This book is about that journey and a guide to help you soar. What will be your first step? Mine was a pair of rose-gold glasses.

Soul Salary Basics:

CHAPTER 1

What Do You Do?

"Nice to meet you. What do you do for a living?"

It is almost automatic to ask. But what lies behind that question? I would like to say it is sheer curiosity and interest in the other person, but is it? Often, it is a way to size a person up.

Notice your automatic thoughts as you read each of the following: CEO, artist, mechanic, technician, landscaper, athlete, doctor, business person, tech company, food industry, tobacco, health care, farming, gun manufacturing. Are you making assumptions? Judgments? Did you subconsciously rank them by success level/potential/morality? That's okay if you did. Deep-rooted societal conditioning is often hard to admit to and recognize.

In many cultures, success is measured by what job you have, what profession you work in, and the financial salary you earn. Success is focused on your title, earnings, clout, work ethic as you hustle and grind, and long work hours. We have become fixated on the value of money and possessions instead of the value of our time, energy, and what our souls desire.

As I was discussing my own inner conflict about expectations with my good friend, we were venting about the exhaustion of trying to be great employees and great moms to our kids plus all the other roles we held. We were so overwhelmed with all of the expectations around us and, frankly, our own expectations of ourselves. We both felt as if we were more than maxed out. I began to question why having a successful and good life was defined as doing it all and having it all. Why can't a good life mean that you have a full and happy soul—not the salary your job is paying you? How high is the salary you are giving to your soul? And that is how the term Soul Salary was born. What if it really is that simple? What if a successful, good life is just doing what aligns with your soul?

Like I mentioned in the intro, Soul Salary is the value your soul receives when your time and energy are spent in alignment with your passions, your life purpose/mission on Earth, and what feeds your soul. Remember that you are the freaking CEO of your life! You have more control than you think, and your job in life is to not disappoint yourself.

If you haven't guessed it yet, in this chapter, I will not ask, "What do you do?" but instead, "Who are you?" Let's get started. Take a minute and ask yourself, "Who are you?"

Who Are You? Exercise:

Fill these in (pick at least seven things you are or aspire to be):

I am _____

I am _____

I am _____

I am _____

I am _____

I am _____

I am _____

Did you say anything like, I am a spouse, a parent, a sibling, someone's child, a (insert job title here)? Those may all be true, but have you ever noticed that you answered "Who are you?" with who you are *for others*? Have you ever taken the opportunity to think about yourself separate from those roles? I want to know: Who are you just for you? What makes you feel alive? Tell *you* about yourself! As English poet Ted Hughes said, "You are who you choose to be."[1]

For example, here is a sampling of who I am/aspire to be:

> ➤ I am centered.
> ➤ I am a free spirit.
> ➤ I am human.
> ➤ I am a gifted healer and guide.

---

[1] Ted Hughes, *The Iron Man*, Revised ed. edition. (Faber & Faber Children's, 2005).

> ➤ I am the sparkling rosé of friends.
> ➤ I am woman.
> ➤ I am powerful.
> ➤ I am me, unapologetically.

The answers to the question "Who are you?" can be used as a motivational and inspirational list for yourself. I suggest posting this list somewhere you can see it every day. Look at it as a list of declarations for yourself.

If you are having trouble coming up with the answer to who you are, you can start with thinking about what your "hype people" say about you. I have a team of hype people (they don't know I call them that!), people who love and support me: my husband, my family, my group of girlfriends, my in-laws, etc. I get to see myself through their eyes as they fill me up with love and joy and keep me on my path—and I do the same for them. They are positive, uplifting, and shower me with celebratory words that I sometimes forget to tell myself. I did not come up with the "I am the sparkling rosé of friends" on my own; it was on a birthday card I received from one of my hype people. Sparkling rosé is bubbly, fun, and girly—how fun is that hype compliment! We all could use some hype people.

If you can't think of any hype people in your life, let me hype you up! You are worthy, you are free, you are amazing and unique, your essence is treasured, and you are *you* unapologetically. Do you need more? Google "I am" statements for more ideas! Let's try the exercise again, focusing on who you are for you and who you aspire to be.

Who Are You? Exercise:

Fill these in (pick at least seven things you are or aspire to be):

I am _____

I am _____

I am _____

I am _____

I am _____

I am _____

I am _____

Reflections:

> Did you change anything from the original list?

_____

_____

_____

> How did that feel?

_____

_____

_____

Was it weird for you to think of yourself in terms of who you are, outside the roles you fulfill for other people? It is so interesting that we can forget parts of ourselves or our dreams in the hustle of life. I am still remembering parts of who I am, and this exercise certainly helped me rediscover a part of me. Do you remember who you are?

CHAPTER 2

What is *Your* Soul Salary?

Are you a High Earner when it comes to Soul Salary? Middle class? Barely making minimum wage? This chapter is focused on figuring out just what *your* Soul Salary is.

Before we dive in with the assessment, take five minutes to try and answer this question: Where do you think you fall in Soul Salary?

Soul Salary Baseline Exercise:

Think about your typical day. How much of your waking time and energy are spent on items that feel joyful and fulfilling? Would you say it is 99 percent? Forty percent? Twenty-five? Two?

Write your answers below for a baseline.

➤ Where do you think you fall in Soul Salary today?

_____

➤ How much of your waking time and energy are spent on things that make you feel joyous and fulfilled?

_____

When I have clients practice this exercise, I am astounded with the vast range in responses. Some people are excited to take the assessment and gain insights—they are often in a learning mindset and ready to make changes. Others are avoidant or in denial—"Well, who really gets to do what they love anyway," "I am fine," "I can't. I am too busy," "I have to do it all, or it won't get done," etc. I totally get the second set of responses. These were my thoughts for years, craving hypervigilant control in the form of endless to-do lists and the comfort of what I knew rather than facing uncomfortable, unknown, and life-altering growth.

Let me make this clear: If you are not ready to go deep, discover, learn, and transform, then you are probably not ready for this book. However, if you are ready to face your discomfort, join me on the other side to feel joy and fulfillment.

I have created an assessment to get specific on what your Soul Salary is, and it can be found at www.JessKaskov.com/SoulSalary. If you would rather be old school and do the assessment magazine-style on paper, I have also included it below. (Side note: Anyone else do the magazine quizzes when they were younger? What Spice Girl are you? Spoiler alert—I am Ginger Spice.) Whether you take the assessment online or in the workbook, make sure and do the Reflections exercise in the workbook.

Your Soul Salary Assessment:

Answer each question below as a yes or no. Pick the answer that comes to mind first so you don't overthink it!

1. Are you taking care of your physical needs (diet, exercise, sleep)? Yes No
2. Are you taking care of your mental and emotional needs? Yes No
3. Do you trust yourself? Yes No
4. Are you content even if you haven't been doing the productive "grind" or "hustling"? Yes No

5. Do you make time for rest and free time? Yes No
6. Do you have plenty of energy for the day? Yes No
7. Are you fulfilled in your life right now? Yes No
8. Do you feel fulfilled in your relationships? Yes No
9. Are you fulfilled in your career? Yes No
10. Are you proud of your life right now? Yes No
11. Are you proud of who you are right now? Yes No
12. Do you feel like you are fulfilling your life purpose? Yes No
13. Do you feel joyful and happy in your life? Yes No
14. Is your life fun? Yes No
15. Do you feel free? Yes No
16. Do you feel lit up, passionate, and on fire? Yes No
17. Do you do what you want/desire to do? Yes No
18. Do you feel free to do what you want? Yes No

Let's score your responses. Tally up all of your "yes" responses for the eighteen questions and see where you fall below:

➤ Sixteen-plus "yes" responses:
  ✦ You are a High Earner! That means you are a person who is very aligned with their joy and likely feel warm, lit up, passionate, useful, and fulfilled.
  ✦ Even scoring as a Higher Earner, I would still suggest moving forward in the book, as it is best to continue to work at Soul Salary to keep High Earner status (or at least read the High Earner chapter!).
➤ Eleven to fifteen "yes" responses:
  ✦ You are middle class. That means you are likely a person who is aware of what brings them joy and fulfillment but has not aligned their time and energy to maximize this.
➤ Ten or less "yes" responses:
  ✦ You are considered at minimum wage. That means you are a person who likely does not know what brings them joy and fulfillment. You are not prioritizing yourself, your joy, your self-love, and/or your self-care.

The questions are also divided into three subcategories for you to assess some ingredients of your Soul Salary:

1. Basic Needs
2. Fulfillment
3. Joy

Total up all of your "yes" responses for questions 1 through 6. These are the Basic Needs questions. Examples in this category include meeting physical, emotional, and mental needs as well as trusting yourself. See below for how you rank in this subcategory.

> High Earner: six "yes" responses
> Middle Class: four to five "yes" responses
> Minimum Wage: three or less "yes" responses

Total up all of your "yes" responses for questions 7 through 12. These are the Fulfillment questions. Examples in this category include fulfillment in relationships, career, and life purpose, as well as pride in your life and who you are. See below for how you rank in this subcategory.

> High Earner: six "yes" responses
> Middle Class: four to five "yes" responses
> Minimum Wage: three or less "yes" responses

Total up all of your "yes" responses for questions 13 through 18. These are the Joy questions. Examples in this category include joy, happiness, fun, passion, freedom, and doing what you want/desire. See below for how you rank in this subcategory.

> High Earner: six "yes" responses
> Middle Class: four to five "yes" responses
> Minimum Wage: three or less "yes" responses

Reflections:

Sit with your results for a moment. Write out any feelings or thoughts that come up for you. This can be a hard moment as you see the numbers on paper, and I honor you for taking a moment to assess and get feedback on where in your life you could feel more joyful, loved, and whole. Remember that you can do the uncomfortable.

> What was your original guess of your Soul Salary?

_____

> Did your guess match or differ from your total Soul Salary score and your Basic Needs, Fulfillment, and Joy subcategory scores? If so, how?

_____

_____

_____

_____

❯ What resonates with you?

_____

_____

_____

_____

❯ What surprises you?

_____

_____

_____

_____

❯ Did this exercise bring up any emotions?

_____

_____

_____

_____

We will use these scores as a baseline of where you are in this moment for your Soul Salary. In the next chapter, we will discuss basic needs as a starting point for making minimum wage in Soul Salary. We will then transition to the Paychecks section of the book, which focuses in detail on the Joy and Fulfillment subcategories of Soul Salary.

I will see you in the next chapter if you are brave enough to go deep and transform. It is time for some productive discomfort.

✦ ✦ ✦ ✦ ✦

CHAPTER 3

Demand Minimum Wage—It's the Law

When I was pregnant with my first child, Riley, I was still trying to work like I had before pregnancy, which meant long hours, being on-call at nights, not breaking for meals (eating during meetings), attending back-to-back meetings, walking the production floor, etc.

In the second trimester, I started having Braxton Hicks contractions (also known as practice labor pains). I would need to sit down and hydrate for the contractions to go away. It got so bad that a few days I had to leave work to go home and rest to stop the contractions. At my next obstetrician doctor appointment, my OB told me she was going to put me on bed rest if I didn't slow down. She actually required me to have work restrictions, and that is when I realized how serious my addiction to work was. Honestly, I was more than embarrassed that it took this slap in the face to open my eyes to how disconnected I was to the needs of my body. I was literally creating another life and still ignoring my needs.

Even if your body isn't creating another life, you need to take care of yourself. Your relationship with yourself and meeting your physical, emotional, and mental needs are the foundation that the rest of your life is built on.

In this chapter, we will discuss meeting your basic needs. I lovingly call this "demanding minimum wage from yourself." It is even a law in the US.

If you are only making minimum wage (or below) in the Basic Needs category, you need to start demanding more from yourself! It is the law to pay your employees at least minimum wage, so do the same for yourself when it comes to meeting your basic needs. You are the CEO of your life; you get to decide your Soul Salary, so "pay" yourself more.

I didn't just come up with this; it's backed by science. Abraham Maslow was an American psychologist who developed Maslow's hierarchy of needs, which is often shown visually as a pyramid (see the next page). The hierarchy emphasizes how you must have basic needs met before you can climb the pyramid to self-actualization. In the "basic needs" foundation of the pyramid, you have physiological needs (air, water, food, shelter, sleep, clothing, etc.) and safety needs (personal security, health, resources, etc.).[2] The same principle applies to Soul Salary, you need to take care of the basic needs of your physical, mental, and emotional parts before you can become a High Earner in Soul Salary. As the saying goes, "when you settle for breadcrumbs, you will always be starving."

---

[2]   Abraham Harold Maslow, "A Theory of Human Motivation," Psychological Review, 50 (1943): pages 370-396, https://doi.org/10.1037/h00543461943.

Maslow's hierarchy of needs

Maslow's hierarchy graphic[3]

Moving beyond Maslow, basic needs are broader than you might think. We hear a lot about physical basic needs, as you need to eat, sleep, drink water, and exercise. In fact, we are bombarded with advice about physical needs—do this diet to lose thirty pounds in ten weeks, drink this much water to have glowing skin, sleep this amount of time (beauty sleep!), do this exact exercise routine to have a six-pack. Our basic needs don't end there, though I couldn't blame you for thinking that.

Our mental and emotional needs are just as foundational, but they are less talked about and often more difficult to figure out.

---

[3] McLeod, S.A., "Maslow's Hierarchy of Needs," [online] Simply Psychology, 2007, http://www.simplypsychology.org/maslow.html, [Accessed January 12, 2023].

Let's talk about all three—physical, mental, and emotional—and discuss some ideas for how to support your basic needs.

The point of this section is not to drive you to be a certain weight, look a certain way, or be able to run a marathon (unless that sounds joyous to you!). The point is to recognize where you would like to better support yourself physically, mentally, and emotionally beyond the bare minimum and to note where your needs are and aren't being met so you know what to work on.

If you don't know where to start, try this challenge. Pause, take a few deep breaths, and take inventory of what you (your body, your mind, your emotions) need today (e.g., sleep, a mental break, a good cry). Commit to taking a step toward a need you have today (e.g., carve out time to take a nap, meditate, watch a sappy movie).

I believe this quote by psychologist Dr. Glenn Patrick Doyle can help us to remember it all starts with a step toward where you want to be:

> Can't clean up the whole room? Clean a corner of it.
> Can't do all the dishes? Do a dish. [...]
> Little wins pave the way for bigger wins.
> 1% beats 0%.[4]

You don't have to solve everything, but do what you can. It's about progress, not perfection—a phrase I will repeat throughout the book. Just keep progressing, and try not to fixate on getting it right the first time.

---

[4] Kathy Muzik, "Something beats nothing—every time," New Path Productivity, accessed on January 20, 2023, https://www.newpathpro.com/blog/something-beats-nothing-every-time.

Body Inventory Exercise:

Pause and take inventory of your body. How do you feel in your body, mind, and emotions today?

➤ Body:

_____

_____

➤ Mind:

_____

_____

➤ Emotions:

_____

_____

What is a step you could take toward supporting your body, mind, and emotions today?

➤ Body:

_____

_____

_____

_____

➤ Mind:

_____

_____

_____

_____

> Emotions:

_____

_____

_____

_____

If you have capacity to go broader than 1 percent and little wins today, reflect on what has worked in the past to support your physical, mental, and emotional needs.

> Body:

_____

_____

_____

_____

_____

> Mind:

_____

_____

_____

_____

_____

> Emotions:

_____

_____

_____

_____

_____

Things that support my physical, mental, and emotional needs include time outdoors (playing with my kids, soaking up the sun, feeling the breeze), quiet time alone (meditation, baths, and journaling), deep connection with friends and family, and movement (living-room dance parties and yoga are my favorites!).

As a reminder, here are the questions you answered in the Basic Needs section of your Soul Salary assessment. Let's look back at your quiz results for questions 1 through 6.

Which questions did you answer "no" to from the Basic Needs section of the Soul Salary assessment?

> Are you taking care of your physical needs (diet, exercise, sleep)?
> Are you taking care of your mental and emotional needs?
> Do you trust yourself?
> Are you content even if you haven't been doing the productive "grind" or "hustling"?
> Do you make time for rest and free time?
> Do you have plenty of energy for the day?

What is just one step you can take to help one "no" turn into a "yes"? This needs to be a one-thing-at-a-time journey to be sustainable, and eventually you *will* move to profound, consistent self-love.

Reflections:

> What is one question from this section that you primarily want to focus on to enhance your basic needs (the one that would make the biggest impact if worked on)?

_____

> Why did you answer "no" to this question? What are the biggest gaps?

_____

_____

_____

_____

_____

> Imagine you are completely fulfilled in this area—visualize it and feel it—and then write ideas to improve this area. Write down all your ideas, even if it includes taking three months of vacation to Fiji. Enjoy the ideation process, even including what you might think is infeasible.

_____

_____

_____

_____

_____

_____

_____

_____

> ➤ Pick one thing to do *this week* and then commit to the next thing and then the next until you are meeting your basic needs at a middle-class level or better!

_____

_____

Nonnegotiables

Part of demanding minimum wage and building your foundation of self-care and self-love is to know your foundational nonnegotiables. When you are job searching and interviewing, you know the variables that help you filter out jobs that are not for you. For example, you may require a certain salary/wage range or minimum, or have deemed it essential to have a certain number of vacation/sick/personal days. Perhaps health care coverage is nonnegotiable, or it is location that is the biggest need. The point is, before you embark on the job search, you decide what your nonnegotiables are. You have also identified the soft lines, or your negotiables, where you *are* willing to give a little if needed.

The same should be true in your life. Know your nonnegotiables. These are your hard boundaries with others and yourself. If you have not identified your nonnegotiables and/or not set clear boundaries around them, it becomes mentally, physically, emotionally, energetically, and time draining. Below are some examples of my nonnegotiables:

> ➤ Physical: I am vegetarian.
> ➤ Mental: I set an intention every day to bring in more presence, peace, and realistic expectations of myself.
> ➤ Emotional: I meditate, journal, and have alone time every day.

> Time: I do not overschedule (e.g., kids get a maximum of two activities each).

> Energy: I do not use more energy in a day than I can recover from in that day.

Another way to consider your nonnegotiables is to look back again at the questions you answered "no" to from the Basic Needs section of the Soul Salary assessment. Consider which nonnegotiables are needed to support your basic needs in that question. I have provided examples below to get your juices flowing:

> Are you taking care of your physical needs (diet, exercise, sleep)?
  ✦ Nonnegotiable: I move my body twenty minutes a day.
  ✦ Negotiable: I get eight hours of sleep, but six to seven are okay.

> Are you taking care of your mental and emotional needs?
  ✦ Nonnegotiable: I sing (read: scream) lyrics to songs on the radio on my commute home to release emotions from work.
  ✦ Negotiable: I meditate for fifteen minutes every day, but any amount of time in meditation is okay.

> Do you trust yourself?
  ✦ Nonnegotiable: I keep my promises to myself when it comes to self-care.
  ✦ Negotiable: I take inventory of myself to assess my needs so I can meet them, but meeting one thing a day (versus all my needs) is okay.

> Are you content even if you haven't been doing the productive "grind" or "hustling"?
  ✦ Nonnegotiable: I will take a break for lunch each day.
  ✦ Negotiable: I will not work more than X hours in a day, but if I sometimes go over that, it is okay.

> Do you make time for rest and free time?
  + Nonnegotiable: I schedule at least one hour of free time per day.
  + Negotiable: I will spend half of my day off on things I enjoy, but if it is less, that is okay.
> Do you have plenty of energy for the day?
  + Nonnegotiable: I take a vitamin every morning.
  + Negotiable: I eat four servings of vegetables a day, but if it is less, that is okay.

Nonnegotiables Exercise:

Write out your nonnegotiables in life—the hard lines. Envision you are looking for your ideal life. What would be the nonnegotiables (whether they are being met currently or not)? Write them below:

My nonnegotiables are:

Physical:

_____

_____

Mental:

_____

_____

Emotional:

_____

_____

Time:

_____

_____

Energy:

_____

_____

Remember: progress, not perfection. So if you don't meet your nonnegotiables every day—let's get real, you won't. I forget my vitamin and overschedule myself sometimes—that is okay. All you have to do is make the choice to start again and again once you notice it to try to improve and keep those boundaries.

It is so critical to take care of ourselves, yet self-care is what we often sacrifice to complete other tasks, duties, expectations, etc. But I know from personal experience this saying rings true: "If you don't make time for your wellness, you will be forced to take time for your illness." It happened to me in my first pregnancy and, if I am speaking honestly, also contributed to mental health episodes in my life. Please don't follow in my footsteps. Learn the lesson I had to keep learning—give yourself radical self-love, unconditional self-love, self-love that is on the brink of indulgence and makes you a little uncomfortable with how much love you are showing yourself. That is my hope for you!

You will know when your basic needs are being met because you are able to recover from your day within the same day (or at least recover from the week in the same week). Once you feel secure that your needs are being met, you are ready to learn about your Soul Salary's paychecks as they relate to joy and fulfillment in your life.

Step 1
Soul Salary Paychecks

CHAPTER 4

Where is Your Joy?

One of my happiest memories is also one when I felt most free. My husband Henry (fiancé at the time) and I were on our last day of vacation in Hawaii and had a few hours before our flight home. Normally, my type-A personality would have us getting to the airport ridiculously early to make sure we didn't miss our flight and we would likely end up waiting hours at the gate. But, in this abnormal state of vacation relaxedness and in a moment of spontaneity, we decided to go to the beach before heading to the airport. The beach was nearly empty with just a few people walking along the shoreline. The waves crashed onto the beach and seemed to be beckoning us to play, so we put on our bathing suits and dove in. The ocean felt warm but also cool compared to the hot sun on our skin. We decided to body surf the waves and immersed ourselves into the flow of the ocean. It was glorious to move with the waves and crash onto the beach as the waves did. I felt like a mermaid as I tasted the saltiness of the water and got sand in my hair. I felt free and joyous.

We didn't have towels or a plan for the stickiness of the ocean that clung to us on a very long flight home. Honestly, we didn't care. It was an ultimate moment of going with the flow of fun. We figured it out and got creative as we went—we took a quick beach shower in our bathing suits and then used my sarong cover-up as our towel. We put our wet items on the car hood to dry, and when it was time to go, we packed them away partially wet. Yes, it wasn't ideal to have some semi-wet stuff in our suitcases, but it was totally worth it to have the spontaneity and thrill of soaking up every last minute of our vacation. To have the moment of not caring what time it was or what our next scheduled activity was and to experience the connection and total presence with each other. I'm smiling and warm just reminiscing!

Joy is brought on by well-being, meeting your desires or being on the path to do so, playing, laughing, etc. Joy is a beautiful feeling that makes your heart sing. It lights you up, and it feels fun. It is a feeling of great pleasure, happiness, and delight. That is why we will start here with our soul searching. Use joy as your map in life.

This chapter and the next two make up the Soul Salary paycheck step of the book, which is focused on finding the unique paychecks that your soul desires. There are two key sources of Soul Salary paychecks: your joy and your fulfillment. This chapter dives into finding your joy using a joy list, which you will make and refer to whenever you need a map back to *your* joy.

To make this joy list, you will first reflect on your past memories and record your happiest ones, then explore why they were your most joyous memories. I shared one of my happiest memories above and the details that made it so—from identifying my senses in the moment (empty beach, hot sun, saltiness of water, sand in my hair), to the connection with my then fiancé, to my feeling of freedom. Focus on transporting yourself back to your moments and reliving the high-vibration joy in the experience. (Side note: You may be thinking, what the heck does high vibration mean? It is "woo-woo" speak for good vibes. It is hippie speak for peace and love. It is metaphysical speak for good and strong energy.)

Joy Moments Exercise:

Spend at least fifteen minutes reminiscing through these questions to get the full effect:

> List moments in your life when you felt the happiest. Go beyond big life events like weddings and births. These can be moments with friends, family, by yourself, traveling, outdoors, indoors, at home, or at work.

_____

_____

_____

_____

_____

_____

_____

_____

_____

> What about each memory made you so happy?

_____

_____

_____

_____

_____

_____

> ❯ Think about the five senses in those moments. Was it the sound of waves, the smell of pie cooking, the taste of fresh-picked fruit, warmth of the sun on your skin, or the view at the top after a mountain hike?

_____

_____

_____

_____

_____

_____

_____

> ❯ Take yourself back to those moments and feel them. Feel the high-vibration energy and think about what you want to take from it going forward to recreate the happiness. Write them here.

_____

_____

_____

_____

_____

Once you are done reminiscing, take some time to answer the following questions to make a complete list of your joy. Write on these questions for at least ten minutes and pour out all the things that make you feel joy from the simple little things to the big and everything in between.

Joy Exercise:

> What brings you joy?

_____

_____

_____

_____

_____

_____

_____

> What makes you feel joyful?

_____

_____

_____

_____

_____

> How do you find joy with each of these?

✦ Friends

_____

_____

✦ Family

_____

_____

✦ Alone time

_____

_____

✦ Self-care/pampering

_____

_____

✦ Work

_____

_____

✦ Personal time

_____

_____

✦ Media

_____

_____

✦ Your environment (indoor or outdoor)

_____

_____

✦ Hobbies and activities

_____

_____

❯ What makes you smile?

_____

_____

_____

_____

❯ What makes you laugh?

_____

_____

_____

_____

> What makes your heart sing?

_____

_____

_____

_____

> What feels like play?

_____

_____

_____

_____

As I was searching for my joy, I started making my own joy list as a reference document. I have it posted in my office to look at whenever I need a reminder or course correction. Below are some things from my joy list. Hopefully it helps spark some more ideas for you!

> **Dancing**—especially in my living room with my kids and husband, making up fun signature-Kaskov-family dances that include butt wiggles and pure silliness.
> **Music**—whether it is chilling with my coffeehouse, acoustic, and meditation music vibes, bopping to pop, or singing along with some country music at the top of my lungs in the car.
> **Books**—reading brings me so much joy. I love books—they are my addiction, hobby, and guilty pleasure. My favorites are self-help books (obviously!).
> **Reflective time alone**—meditation, yoga, and journaling are my favorite reflective time tools.

> **Water**—I am convinced that I was a mermaid in another life for how much I feel at peace in the water.

> **Warmth**—warm and snuggly on a winter or rainy day with a big sweater, wool cabin socks, blankets, a fire, and hot tea or the sun-kissed warmth of summer. I have different candles that I light based on my mood. I even have a candle with crystals and dried lavender because why not?

> **Laughing**—belly laughing with friends and family to the point of feeling like I got an ab workout. I will say that I am also known for my laugh. I have gotten more than one comment on my laugh's uniqueness (read: loud and boisterous).

> **Connection**—vulnerable, deep conversations with friends and even strangers light me up. Inspiring and supporting others through sharing my story and my experiences.

> **Creativity**—writing, painting, creating dream catchers, cross-stitch, to name a few.

> **Holiday season**—I keep all of my Christmas cards on a bulletin board in my kitchen year-round and start listening to Christmas music way too early in the year, but I enjoy the feeling of the holidays and want to relish in it.

Now that you've seen mine, let's work on making your own!

Your Joy List Exercise:

Review your responses in the Joy Moments and Joy exercises and write down the similarities and items you feel give you the most joy. This is your joy list!

_____

_____

_____

_____

_____

_____

_____

_____

_____

I would suggest posting your joy list somewhere you can see it as a reminder to bring joy into your day (or where it is readily accessible to reference when needed). Remember to find your joy, hold on to it, crave it, and actively seek it out. Do this by increasing your joyful moments by an interval of time each week. Start with a few extra minutes—yes, you may need to cut binging on social media slightly or wake up a few minutes early or actually take a lunch or snack break from work to do this. Remember, these can be baby steps to more joy. Take it as slow as you need to to adjust to making joy a priority.

When you add joy and hold space for it, you truly live up to "finding joy in the journey." Who doesn't like a little sprinkle of joy in their lives? Don't forget the feelings you felt when you wrote about your happiest moments—who wouldn't want more of that? Why not have fun while we learn and grow? We are meant to have fun and find joy; in fact, I believe it is one of the main purposes of our lives. So, I plan to continue to "find joy in the journey." Will you?

Remember to go back to your list often. The items on your list are some of the paychecks your soul desires. In the next chapter, we explore another aspect of your Soul Salary paychecks: your fulfillment of your desired legacy or life purpose.

CHAPTER 5

What is Your Legacy?

What is your legacy? When I first thought about this question, I will be honest and say that I really didn't know and may have even said something like, "Whoa, that is deep." I hadn't thought about my legacy much, and when I paused and reflected, I realized that much of what I was doing in my day-to-day was not aligned with the legacy I wanted to leave, or a purpose that felt authentic and fulfilling to me.

Understanding and living the legacy you were meant to leave is directly related to your feelings of fulfillment. Your Soul Salary increases when you feel more joy and fulfillment (and vice versa). They are perfectly correlated. You just made your joy list in the last chapter, and in this chapter, you are going to make your legacy statement. I know this is a deep topic, but don't worry, I will help you break this down!

My first attempt to answer the question, "What is your legacy?" led me to create a legacy statement. My first legacy statement was "Be you unapologetically," reminding myself that my legacy was being and showing my true self without embarrassment and without making myself small. After many more iterations (some samples include: "to-be list, not to-do list" and "Discover. Be. Love."), my legacy statement continued to evolve until I landed on a legacy statement that inspired me to my core: "I make a profound impact on the world by spreading love and joy broadly, starting with me." As you can see, your legacy statement can be long or short. It can be for this season you are in or for your whole life.

Through books, we have the ability to time travel, and although I may not get to meet my great-great-grandchildren, they will still have me in their lives thanks to this book. I also want this book to broadly impact the world and guide my readers to more joyful and fulfilling lives, so they can then spread more love and joy into the world. I wish for this book to be reflective of my legacy statement and what I am remembered for. As I write this, I am getting chills—a telltale sign that I am on the right track. This legacy statement makes me feel passionate and lit up with love. When you get a feeling like this, you know that what you desire is in alignment with your true self and life purpose.

The legacy statement can be used as a mantra, a guiding phrase, an inspirational memo to yourself when you are feeling stuck, etc. It can help you make decisions as you ask yourself, *is this in alignment with my legacy statement?* It can help you stay motivated by reciting it every day to yourself. It can hold you accountable to your purpose.

Create your own legacy statement! First, let's explore the past and what has made you proud in your life so far. I want to put emphasis on the word *you*. What are *you* most proud of in your life so far? Your response may or may not align with what society, your parents, your partner, your siblings, your friends, your coworkers, or anyone else would say is the most impressive or most worthy of pride in your life so far. This is about your personal sense of pride because we are all unique, and your assignment in life is to not disappoint *yourself*, not to *not* disappoint others. As you do this exercise, similar to the Joy Moments exercise in the previous chapter, focus on transporting yourself back to that moment and reliving the high-vibration pride in the experience.

Pride Moments Exercise:

> What are *you* most proud of in your life so far?

_____

_____

_____

_____

_____

_____

_____

_____

> List those moments in your life where you felt this pride. Go beyond big life events like weddings and births. These can be moments with friends, family, by yourself, traveling, outdoors, indoors, at home, or at work.

_____

_____

_____

_____

_____

➤ What about each memory made you feel so proud?

_____

_____

_____

_____

_____

_____

_____

➤ Take yourself back to those moments and feel them. Feel the
high-vibration energy and think about what you want to take
from it going forward in your legacy. Write them here.

_____

_____

_____

_____

_____

_____

When I asked these questions to one of my close friends, who
has a doctorate, birthed her children naturally (without drugs!),
and breastfed her kids until they were over twelve months
while still working—all of which are certainly impressive—she
did not list any of these as what she was personally most proud
of. This example is a good one to show the difference between
what you are personally proud of versus our conditioning of
what society says is something to be proud of.

This reflection exercise on what you are proud of shows you
what aligns with your soul's essence and your personal values.

Now that you have looked at your past prideful moments, let's take some time to do another exercise on legacy and answer a series of questions on what your legacy is. Free write for at least ten minutes to make sure you dig deeply and empty out your thoughts. If you run out of ideas during that time, go back to your answers and ask yourself, *why?* And keep asking why until you have gotten to a very heart-based answer.

Legacy Exercise:

What is your legacy? Answer these questions:

> What do you want to be remembered for?

_____

_____

_____

_____

_____

_____

✦ Why?

_____

_____

> When you leave this life, what do you want to leave behind in terms of your legacy?

_____

_____

_____

_____

_____

✦ Why?

_____

_____

❯ What do you want other people to say about you at your funeral? If you could write your eulogy, what would you want to be in there?

_____

_____

_____

_____

_____

✦ Why?

_____

_____

❯ Why?

_____

_____

❯ Why?

_____

_____

❯ Why?

_____

_____

Initially I knew I wanted to write a book. Why? Because it was on my bucket list. I then asked myself,

Why?

> I want to use the book to start a new career where I help others.

Why?

> I want to share my story and experience with the world to help other people.

Why?

> I have found love, joy, and fulfillment for myself, and I want to spread it broadly to others.

Why?

> Loving, joyful, and fulfilled people elevate others, and it is a domino effect, which means each person who elevates themselves in these ways makes a profound impact on the world by starting a chain reaction.

See how my legacy went deeper and deeper into a loving intention as I repeatedly asked, *why?* It went from "it is on my bucket list" to "elevating others and changing the world." This is a profound exercise if you take the time to get to a powerful root that motivates you to the core.

Now that you have completed the two exercises, review your responses and determine the similarities and items you feel most passionate about. These are the legacy you want to leave and are also what your soul desires for fulfillment.

Then, work on clearly and concisely expressing these similarities in a short phrase or sentence. The goal is to make a legacy statement that can be easily remembered and affirms your legacy aspirations. As author James Redfield says, "Where intention goes, energy flows." This statement urges you to be intentional and purpose driven so your energy flows to where you want it to.

These statements can be a specific intention for your phase of life (e.g., "have courage and be kind") or more of a reflection of your true nature (e.g., "I am love and joy"). Both are welcome and wonderful as legacy statements. And as with anything, this can get more specific or more general and edited over time as you change and develop. Do not feel like this needs to be your final legacy statement—it is dynamic.

Legacy Statement Exercise:

> ➤ Review your responses from the Pride Moments exercise and Legacy exercise and determine the similarities and items you feel most passionate about. What are they?

_____

_____

_____

_____

_____

_____

_____

_____

_____

> Create your legacy statement. Try many iterations until you get the one that resonates the most.

_____

_____

_____

_____

_____

_____

_____

Reflections:

Read through your responses to these exercises.

> Is there anything that surprises you?

_____

_____

_____

_____

> How do you feel reading through this list? Nostalgia, pride, contentment, drive to do more, disappointment? Notice your emotions. All are valid and allowed.

_____

_____

_____

_____

Being in alignment with your legacy statement is how you feel fulfillment in your life. Your Soul Salary is the value your soul receives when your time and energy are spent in alignment with your passions, your life purpose/mission on Earth, and what feeds your soul. Your joy list and your legacy statement *are* your passions, your life purpose, and what feeds your soul. They are what your soul desires and are the paychecks for your Soul Salary.

Note if there are common themes between the joy list and legacy statement.

_____

_____

_____

_____

_____

_____

_____

_____

_____

These themes are where you have the largest "income" potential in your Soul Salary paycheck since they bring you joy and feelings of fulfillment (two for one!). The next chapter helps you visualize your ideal job (scratch that—your ideal *life!*).

✦ ✦ ✦ ✦ ✦

CHAPTER 6

Your Ideal ~~Job~~ Life

The year I wrote this book, my oldest son (seven years old), Riley, actually helped me make the decision to take the leap and pursue my dream of becoming an author. For Mother's Day, the school gave Riley a card to decorate and fill in. The prompt: "My wish for mom." His response: "I wish for you to feel free." He gifted me this Mother's Day card along with a coupon book for snuggles and hugs. Cue waterworks. It felt like such a blessed message for the road ahead and is a core value I carry now. I am free to be myself and take paths that feel joyful and fulfilling even if they are out of my comfort zone and sometimes terrifying. I wish for you to be free to pursue your desires and callings in whatever way you wish.

In fact, I wish for you to remember that you are already free. You are the CEO of your life—you just need to act like it! In this chapter, we will do a visualization of your ideal ~~job~~ life. This is a visualization you can do anytime to raise your vibration, to align yourself with your dreams, and to help you manifest your way there. Visualization literally reprograms your brain to be in alignment with your visualization. If you can believe it, you can *be* it. Before we dive into the guided visualization, I have a few pieces of advice on how to proceed with the work in the rest of the book, and especially as you visualize your ideal life:

① **Don't be afraid to be different (i.e., weird).** My fourth-grade teacher was a wise woman. When a kid in our class called me weird, she interjected and said, "Weird is a compliment." Who wants to be normal when you can be your unique self? I think everyone is meant to be their own one-of-a-kind self, so don't be afraid to think and be outside the box.

② **Dream without limits.** In my childhood bedroom, I had an armoire with stars and the moon on it and this quote from author Norman Vincent Peale: "Shoot for the moon. Even if you miss, you'll land among the stars."[5] Get in the mindset of dreaming big! Don't make yourself small. Shoot for the moon, for the stars, for outside this galaxy, and beyond!

③ **Share your dreams** with people you trust. There is power in saying your dreams out loud and setting them in motion through your words and intentions. In this chapter, we are going to use your newfound list of the paychecks your soul desires (your joy list and legacy statement) to visualize and write out your ideal job (i.e., your ideal life).

Let's start with the visualization. Sit up in your chair and close your eyes. Take some deep breaths until you feel calm and grounded. Visualize that you have your ideal life. What does a perfect day look like to you? Sit with it for a few minutes and enjoy the sensory experience of living the life you desire. Take a final deep breath and open your eyes.

---

[5] Ron Elving, "Norman Vincent Peale Was A Conservative Hero Known Well Beyond His Era," NPR, Accessed on January 20, 2023, https://www.npr.org/2020/07/24/894967922/ norman-vincent-peale-was-a-conservative-hero-known-well-beyond-his-era.

Visualization Exercise:

Write your reflections:

I saw:

_____

I heard:

_____

I smelled:

_____

I tasted:

_____

I felt:

_____

When I did this exercise while I was working my corporate engineering job, I saw a totally different experience than my life at the time. I dreamed of a life as a creator, writer, and coach.

> I saw: myself reading with a blanket by the fire, writing in my home office or outside, having deep conversations and connections with people, and myself as a playful, loving mom and wife who goes with the flow and feels wonder and joy.

> I heard: calming music (meditation, piano, acoustic), laughing.

> I smelled: scented candles, sage, incense, hot tea (I am talking about a concoction—blending different tea, lemon, honey—all the works and decadence).

> I tasted: scones, sparkling water, lots of tea and H2O.

> I felt: warm, cozy, happy, at ease, free, loved and loving, creative energy running through me, supported.

Now that you have done the visualization and written your experience, let's make a list of the job requirements/prerequisites to be living 100 percent in this ideal life.

Let's take my visualization, for example. For this to come true, here are a few things I needed to do to meet the job requirements/ prerequisites from the place I was when I did the visualization:

> Quit my corporate job.
> Study to enhance my writing/creating skills.
> Get certified in life coaching.
> Continue to heal myself and make changes in my life for my joy and fulfillment.
> Stock up on tea, scented candles, and incense.
> Organize and declutter my office and home so it feels warm and cozy and I can feel at ease.

Other common themes I have seen:

> Ask for and give yourself what you need.
> Ask others for help. They say, "It takes a village," so use the village (even if you aren't raising kids, as the quote originates from, all of us need a village!).
> Face your fears.
> Retrain your brain to govern negative thoughts and beliefs.
> Research and come up with creative solutions.

Are you ready to design your life? Let's go!

Job Requirements Exercise:

What would you need to do to meet the job requirements/prerequisites to live 100 percent in this ideal ~~job~~ life?

_____

_____

_____

_____

_____

_____

_____

_____

_____

_____

_____

Where in your life are you already working on some of these, or have you done so in the past? For example, when I was doing a mass decluttering of the house (see point above about making sure my office and home where warm and cozy and made me feel at ease!), I was going through boxes and boxes of memorabilia and found a poetry award I won in middle school for my poem on prejudice. I didn't even remember this award, but it was so amazing to find this tidbit about how I used to write/create when I was a kid, especially as I am rediscovering that part of myself now. Similarly, this memory reminded me that as a kid I used to stay up late on my mom's old typewriter and type out stories I made up. It is funny how I had forgotten these little glimpses of myself until I started to dive deeply into soul searching! Going through that cluttered storage, I found a treasure in the form of a reminder of who I am. I hope this exercise helped you find some reminders of who you are.

We have created our joy list, legacy statement, ideal life visualization, and job requirements. These are your paychecks and your ideal "job." Now we want to increase your paychecks with raises and promotions to get you closer to High Earner status in Soul Salary and closer to your ideal ~~job~~ life. In the next section of the book, we focus on step 2, giving yourself raises and promotions.

Step 2
Raises and Promotions

CHAPTER 7

Give Yourself a Raise!

I increased my Soul Salary paycheck by decreasing my financial paycheck. I know that sounds counterintuitive, but I realized through some deep soul searching that in order to give myself minimum soul wage and add more joy and fulfillment in my life, I needed to give myself a Soul Salary raise to have more time to pursue my self-care and passions. After completing night school to become a certified life coach, I decided to propose a part-time arrangement with the company I worked for. It is *not* common for supply chain professionals to be part-time employees, and I was nervous to ask. I practiced my script multiple times by myself and with my mentors before I went in for the pitch. It was the first time I had asked for something big like this in my fifteen years in the industry. The long-awaited moment came, and to my surprise, my manager said yes and we got to work on reshuffling within the team so I could have Monday afternoons and Fridays off of work. You never know what is possible unless you ask. These are examples of (admittedly large) Soul Salary raises.

After my ideal life visualization, I started to move toward that ideal with the above series of raises, each aligned with my basic needs, joy, fulfillment, or some combination. First, as mentioned, I enrolled in night school and earned my certificate in life coaching. This aligned with the joy I find in deep, personal connection with others. Next, I became a part-time employee. This aligned with my basic needs (radical self-care, personal growth, and reflection), nonnegotiables (I do not overschedule, daily alone time), and time to pursue my passions (particularly writing and journaling). There were many other steps in that journey, but I wanted to show you a couple examples of my saga of Soul Salary exploration and personal raises.

Rest assured, raises don't need to be as dramatic as mine or revolve around a total career change. A raise in your Soul Salary could be in smaller steps, like buying yourself flowers each week, going for hikes on the weekends, booking a trip, treating yourself to eating out once a week, etc. You alone get to decide what will raise your Soul Salary paychecks and your capacity to take action where you are at today.

Speaking of raises, when I did a quick Google search on negotiating a raise, I found (and read) a large sampling of articles. I have taken the themes of these how-to articles and listed them below as reference as you embark on asking yourself for a raise.

(1) Gather positive feedback.
   > Our focus should be on things about ourselves that we are proud of. Re-read your notes from the Pride Moments exercise in Chapter 5 to remember this positive feedback you gifted yourself.
   > Find your hype people like we talked about in Chapter 1.

(2) Use data.

> The key is to know your worth and the value you bring, which is tied to your own self-worth. Remember, we demand minimum wage as the bare minimum by taking care of our physical, mental, and emotional basic needs as well as knowing our nonnegotiables (Chapter 3). This is the data you need to work to give yourself a raise.

(3) Remember what you bring to the table.

> We worked through this when writing your legacy statement in Chapter 5. Your legacy is what you will bring to your life and leave for the world.

(4) Ideate on why your boss should give you more money.

> *You are the boss, the CEO*—this is all about self-worth and self-love. You only need to convince yourself that you are worthy of a higher Soul Salary (more joy and fulfillment). Remember your joy list and that you are worthy of feeling joy (Chapter 4). If the reason for doing something is just that it makes your heart sing, then your boss (i.e., you) should want to give you more of it!

(5) Develop a goal and timetable.

> In this chapter, we will discuss the use of S.M.A.R.T. goals—specific, measurable, achievable, relevant, timely—to get clear on what you want and how to get it.

(6) Practice asking for what you want.

> Visualize getting what you want (remember your ideal life visualization in Chapter 6) and act like you already have everything you desire. Also remember who you are! Think back to Chapter 1 where you declared who you are.

> With this clarity (from your ideal life visualization) and confidence, get clear on what help and support you need. These are ideas where you can ask for what you want.

⑦ Finally, as author Napoleon Hill states, "Whatever your mind can conceive and believe, it can achieve."[6]

> *Conceive* the ideal life you want, *believe* you can increase your Soul Salary to get there, and allow yourself to *achieve* it.

As you can see, the advice that is given in the professional context can be used in your Soul Salary raise prep as well!

There are two ways to increase your Soul Salary:

1. **Increase your soul paychecks** (add more time and energy doing things from your joy list or your legacy statement).
2. **Reduce your bills** (reduce Joy Killers and Soul Suckers—we will talk about these in the next section of the book).

Right now, let's talk about the former—raising your paychecks, because you have earned a raise! We will start with a series of questions to brainstorm how you can raise your Soul Salary. When you do this exercise, assume you have complete freedom, you can break any rules you want to, and there are no consequences for any actions you list. Think big *and* think small. In this ideation, you can pick things that are additions to your life (e.g., sign up for a painting class) or subtractions to your life (e.g., resign as president of the school PTO). We can always start with the smaller steps (Soul Salary raises) if

---

6   Napoleon Hill, *Think and Grow Rich*, Later Printing Edition. (Chartwell Books, 2015).

you aren't ready for the big steps (Soul Salary promotions). However, this exercise is often where bold ideas come up, so let them flow. It does not mean you have to take action on these; it simply allows for creative solutions to emerge as you understand your underlying desires.

Raise Brainstorm Exercise:

Let's start brainstorming how you can raise your Soul Salary. Answer these questions:

> What is the most significant thing you could do for your soul?

_____

_____

_____

_____

_____

> What is the best thing that can happen for you?

_____

_____

_____

_____

_____

> What are some things you could do to advance your life?

_____

_____

_____

_____

_____

> ➤ As you review your list/answers to the questions above, look back at your joy list/legacy statement. Is there anything you would add to the list to incorporate those items into your life more?

_____

_____

_____

_____

> ➤ Look at your ideal life description. Is there anything you would add to the list to incorporate that aspiration into your life more?

_____

_____

_____

_____

> ➤ Anything else to add?

_____

_____

_____

Below are a few examples from my clients (from life-altering changes to smaller upleveling changes):

> ➤ Cut out toxic friends/relationships.
> ➤ Stop drinking.
> ➤ Move to another state/country.
> ➤ Stop binging screen time (Netflix, social media, etc.).
> ➤ Trade services (trade babysitting with another family so each family's parents get time away without kids).

> Ask your partner, friends, or family to support you more (chores, hosting holiday dinners, driving the kids around).
> Hire help (grocery delivery, therapist, nanny, babysitter, coach, personal trainer, nutritionist).
> Do the things on your bucket list now.
> Go back to school/study something new.
> Ask for more time off or reduce hours at work (unpaid vacation, negotiate more paid vacation).
> Hire more staff for your business.
> Quit your job/apply for a different role.
> Start over.
> Homeschool your kids.
> Travel the world.

Your Raise Brainstorming exercise is your list of ideas to give yourself raises and promotions, now and in the future. We start with one raise at a time and, once achieved, look to get the next raise, and so on. Eventually, the low-hanging fruit will be gone and you will go from giving yourself raises to giving yourself a promotion—which tend to be more difficult decisions and bigger changes. We will talk about promotions in the next chapter. For now, remember this famous quote from minister and activist Martin Luther King Jr., "You don't have to see the whole staircase, just take the first step."[7] Let's take the first step.

Now that we have done the dreaming part, let's get to the practical execution. Looking at your list, color-code the ideas you could do right now, this month, this year, the next five years, and beyond. This color-coding acts as a rough map for timing the items on your list. This is a first pass, and things

---

7 Teresa Pearson, "You Don't Have to See the Whole Staircase," Sage Journals, Accessed on January 20, 2023, https://journals.sagepub.com/doi/full/10.1177/2325160313508269.

can always change as far as timing, the items on the list, your desires, etc. We need to start somewhere, and where you are right now is a reflection of the Soul Salary raise map you just developed. We will start there!

Looking at your list, answer the following:

> What are some things you could do right now, or are willing to do right now, to give yourself a raise in Soul Salary? (Highlight or mark them green.)
> What are some things you could do this month? (Highlight or mark them pink.)
> What are some things you could do this year? (Highlight or mark them orange.)
> What are some things you could do in the next five years? (Highlight or mark them blue.)

Now that you have seen some examples and color-coded your list, you will make an intentional decision to do one of the things to raise your Soul Salary. Start by setting a S.M.A.R.T. goal—specific, measurable, achievable, relevant, timely—to get clear on what you want, how to get it, and what help you need to make this happen.

Here is an example of a S.M.A.R.T. goal:

I want to publish a self-help book by the end of the year. I will start with writing a draft, then move on to editing by hiring a professional editor, and then publishing. I hope this book will make a profound impact on the world as I follow my passion of writing.

Now let's break it down into the S.M.A.R.T. framework:

> **Specific** goal: *I want to publish a self-help book.*
> How will it be **Measured** (how will you know you have been successful): *Publish.*
> Is this goal **Achievable** (if not, break it into smaller steps) and how: *I will start with writing a draft, then move on to editing by hiring a professional editor, and then publishing.*
> Is this goal **Relevant** to increasing your Soul Salary paychecks by raising your joy (joy list), fulfillment (legacy statement), and/or basic needs and nonnegotiables? *I hope this book will make a profound impact on the world as I follow my passion of writing.*
> When will you reach this goal? Make it **Timely**: *By the end of the year.*

Don't forget to invite others to have a role in your "company" (i.e., your life). There is a lot of power in asking for help and allowing for others to be a part of your dream and vision. Happy imagining and growing!

A few examples of help:

> Learning material (e.g., a book, course, teacher).
> Support from others (e.g., family member, travel agent, counselor, joining a club).
> Time (e.g., vacation time, time without kids).

Raise S.M.A.R.T. Goal Exercise:

Now that you have seen some examples, gathered some helpers, and color-coded your list, let's make an intentional decision to do one of the things to raise your Soul Salary today. Set your first goal below:

> What is one thing you will do first to raise your Soul Salary? Use the S.M.A.R.T (specific, measurable, achievable, relevant, timely) goal framework:

* Specific goal:

_____

_____

_____

* How will it be Measured (how will you know you have been successful):

_____

_____

* Is this goal Achievable (if not, break it into smaller steps) and how:

_____

_____

_____

* Is this goal Relevant to increasing your Soul Salary paychecks by raising your joy (joy list), fulfillment (legacy statement) and/or basic needs and nonnegotiables?

_____

_____

_____

* When will you reach this goal? Make it Timely:

_____

_____

> ❯ What help do you need to make this happen? How are you
> going to make space for this change in your life?

_____

_____

_____

_____

_____

Planning is awesome and helps to get the juices flowing and make your dream a reality. However, a big mistake I have seen is not being flexible or open to creative solutions. Often, we have a vision of exactly what our future should be and do not allow ourselves to be open to our dreams coming to us in a different form than originally envisioned. Stay open and flexible as long as the solution presenting itself is in alignment with your soul, your joy, and your fulfillment.

Congratulations on your first Soul Salary raise. Now let's get you that much-deserved promotion!

CHAPTER 8

Time for a Promotion

Painting by numbers has been one of my outlets. I painted one that felt particularly special. It was the birth flower of April, which is daisies (April is the special month where I became a mother). It shows three flowers in multiple stages: the bud, the flower in full bloom, and the wilting flower. Not to get too poetic, but I felt it was a fitting metaphor for ourselves. We are always growing into new forms and releasing what no longer serves us, while also being in full bloom at that exact moment.

As I wrote and edited this book, I found I was also editing myself. I was doing the exercises I developed to continue to grow even though I had done all of these exercises before. That is the point, isn't it—to hold space to be all three flowers, to keep growing the flower buds and pruning the wilting flowers while also remaining in full bloom in the present. Easier said than done, but I am rooting for you (pun intended)!

When I started on my personal Soul Salary journey, I was enjoying giving myself raises. I increased my Soul Salary paychecks, as mentioned before, by learning more about something that brought me joy and fulfillment. I went to life coaching school at night and became certified and moved to part time at my corporate job. These were big improvements in my life, but I felt these were more raises versus promotions in my Soul Salary journey.

Promotions in Soul Salary are the next level beyond the lower hanging fruit and safer/easier decisions to make. My raises were more of a dimmer versus an on-off switch. One of my Soul Salary promotions was when I quit my corporate job completely and took the leap to follow my heart and become 100 percent self-employed.

A Soul Salary promotion requires big decisions and uncomfortable life changes. As author John A. Shedd wrote, "A ship in harbor is safe, but that is not what ships are built for."[8] A promotion is normally a choice between a comfort zone and a new adventure, between convenient, secure, and approved and the path your heart is drawn to even if it is illogical and risky. Choose your truth, your inner voice, your intuition, and use your gut! There are always more than two choices. It is not black or white; there is always at least one gray option too. Get creative in your solutions. In the end, you get to decide what is considered a Soul Salary raise or promotion for your life, but those are my general guidelines for my personal Soul Salary journey. No matter what you call them, the goal is the same— increase your Soul Salary.

Below are some examples of promotions:

> Changes in your family (e.g., fostering, adopting, pregnancy, pets).
> Moving (e.g., location, buildings, new roommates).

---

[8]   John A. Shedd, *Salt from My Attic*, Original Edition. (Mosher Press, 1928).

> Leaving or starting a relationship (e.g., marriage, divorce/ breakup, friendship, cutting off communication with a toxic family member).
> Career/job changes (e.g., reduced hours, increased hours, company change, industry change, new career, going back to school).
> Inviting others into your "company"/life by asking them to have a role (e.g., joining a club, hiring an employee, pitching what you want to your boss and asking them to help you get there).
> Big lifestyle changes (e.g., from couch potato to marathon runner, from meat and potatoes to vegan diet, from indulgent to sober).
> Taking risks (e.g., self-employment, living off the grid, vulnerably sharing your trauma story).

Hopefully this helped get your juices flowing for the exercise ahead, where you will answer open-ended questions to determine how far you are willing to go for your Soul Salary. Remember that there are always potential risks when taking big leaps and changing your life as well as benefits. In this book, I give you space to write out the risks and benefits you see with one of your promotion ideas and to brainstorm ways to eliminate or mitigate the risks.

Promotions Exercise

Answer these open-ended questions to see where you are at right now:

> What is your Soul Salary worth to you?

_____

_____

_____

> How far are you willing to go to raise your Soul Salary and become a High Earner?

_____

_____

_____

> Pick one idea for a promotion and write the benefits and risks.

Promotion:

_____

_____

Benefits:

_____

_____

_____

_____

Risks:

_____

_____

_____

_____

> What are some actions you can take to eliminate or mitigate the risks?

_____

_____

_____

_____

_____

_____

_____

A little while before I finished my book, I was brainstorming about my new career identity and was feeling that finishing my book was the next thing to do in this entrepreneurship journey. My youngest son (five years old), Parker, unknowingly confirmed it for me. That week, he brought home an "I am an author" crown from completing his first writing module at school. I chose to embrace that very clear sign and start giving myself that exact affirmation: "I am an author!" Parker even let me keep the crown in my office among my favorite self-help books.

Yes, my book wasn't a finished manuscript yet, but I am an author—I wrote a whole book! The next promotion at that time was publishing it to share my dreams with the world.

You are free. Trust yourself—you have to believe it to be it. Experiment and do some trial and error. Debrief your decisions and pivot as needed. No one expects you to get it right the first time. The only failure is if you stop trying.

As author Glennon Doyle says, "This life is mine alone. So, I have stopped asking people for directions to places they've never been. There is no map. We are all pioneers."[9] You are always creating, whether it is by default or by design. You choose to be on cruise control or to be the dang driver. Remember, not doing anything is also a choice.

In the next section (step 3), we move from paychecks to diving into our Soul Salary bills, which I lovingly refer to as Joy Killers and Soul Suckers.

---

[9]   Glennon Doyle, *Untamed*, Hardcover edition. (New York: The Dial Press, 2020), page 60.

Step 3
Soul Salary Bills

CHAPTER 9

Joy Killers

Do you remember all that wonder and pure joy of being a kid? Chasing butterflies, collecting rocks and seashells and all bits and pieces of nature, dancing without inhibitions, singing at the top of your lungs, or literally stopping to smell the roses. Take a minute and sit with it. Visualize your wonder. Visualize your pure-joy moments of childhood.

I remember talking and singing all the time (let's be honest, I talked everyone's ear off). I loved exploring nature and was in awe of the new things I found—a feather, a view, a stream, or catching a fish with my dad. I loved being creative—crafts with my mom, creating plays to perform with my sister, or weaving with a loom. I even took up rug hooking for a while (I made a Winnie the Pooh mini-rug). Happiness seems to come naturally for children. When do we learn unhappiness, I wonder?

No matter how happy we are as children, as we grow up, we start to dim our light to fit in and meet others' (and our own) expectations of ourselves. We start to get categorized—she is good at math, he is good at sports, they are the well-behaved kids, he is the rowdy kid of the class, or she is the tomboy. We become self-conscious of the parts of us that are different from the norm, and slowly, the sense of wonder is replaced by a desire to follow the group. The joy dims, and we only allow it to exist when it is joy that is accepted by our surroundings and culture. Maybe instead of dancing without inhibitions, we start to only do the trending dance (e.g., the dab, the floss, etc.). Or instead of singing at the top of our lungs, we hum along or tap our fingers. Instead of chasing butterflies, we mildly observe their presence or miss them completely. And instead of screaming with joy at a milestone met, we gently clap our hands or nod a "thanks" to the recognition of achievement.

I understand and honor that being a misfit and being bullied is incredibly hard to endure. When I was in middle school, I ran for class president. I went all in. I made signs and buttons, and as I passed out the buttons, everyone said they planned to vote for me. I felt like I was definitely going to win the vote, but regardless, I was a nervous mess as they were announcing the winners.

Not only was I not the winner for class president, I also found out that people were only saying they would vote for me as part of a cruel joke. My classmates made me believe I was getting their votes as a trick. It was, sadly, one of the most memorable moments when I significantly dimmed my light. I became self-conscious and tried to blend in by changing my clothes to neutral colors versus wearing the bold colors I normally donned (I even had a rainbow-sequined vest—needless to say, that didn't make the cut anymore). I survived that year by being a chameleon. Thankfully the next year my family moved to a new state, and I was able to start over with a new school. I can also proudly say that I was president of many organizations after middle school (take that, bullies!).

But it continues onward from childhood to high school, to dating, to your job, and beyond. This shaping of ourselves to others' expectations to fit in—people-pleasing, creating expectations that are out of touch with our true self's expectations, perfectionism, having a need for control, etc.—can continue for our whole lives. We often seek to meet or exceed expectations to avoid criticism and bullying or to gain praise and accolades. We begin to tie our worth to external sources and whether we get praise for what we did, versus knowing that we are worthy just as we are today.

Somewhere along my life journey, I started to care deeply about others' expectations and took them on as my own. I knew I was supposed to make a good living, pick a good college and prestigious major, get honors, work hard, and overall, be impressive. I made some big life decisions based on others' expectations of me, as well as my unrealistic and out-of-touch expectations of myself. Even though, as a child, I wanted to be a teacher, I moved my path toward engineering. I chose a top engineering school, graduated as a female engineer with highest honors (women only made up 17 percent of the college of engineering at the time), and worked for a Fortune 500 company, getting promotions at an impressive cadence. The external praise and accolades became addictive—how can I get more, be better, succeed higher? When would it be enough? I became impressive to societal standards, but I was missing out on joy, because what I was doing wasn't aligned with my true self. I am not an engineer at heart (although I do love processes), no matter how good I am at it. I am a thought leader, a guide, and a teacher at my core.

Don't get me wrong—when I look back on those choices, while I know they may not have been perfectly aligned with my true self, I acknowledge that the college I went to is how

I met my husband, the career I chose is how I realized that my legacy is how I touch other people's lives, and the major I chose and the honors I received gave me enormous confidence in my abilities. I am proud of myself for the things I have accomplished and for the lessons they have taught me about life, people, and priorities, but this saying sums up the lesson: "Just because you *can* do something doesn't mean you *should*."

As you raise your Soul Salary, your joy and fulfillment are also increasing. That is why as we look at our Soul Salary paychecks, we focus on these two. The last sections were focused on finding the unique paychecks that your soul desires. We have two key sources of paychecks: your joy list and your desired legacy.

Just like in the real world, no matter how many raises you get, if your bills are too big, your net income isn't very high. This section focuses on Soul Salary bills, which are things that take away from your paychecks. I will also refer to bills as "Joy Killers" and "Soul Suckers." They are out of alignment with your life purpose, passion, and what lights you up. We will explore what these bills are for your individual soul and learn how to reduce these bills so you don't feel like a "poor soul." Let's start with the Joy Killers.

As research professor Brené Brown wrote in her book *The Gifts of Imperfection,* "Fitting in is becoming who you think you need to be in order to be accepted. Belonging is being your authentic self and knowing that no matter what happens, you belong to you."[10] The top two Joy Killers are taking on other's expectations and taking on your own out-of-touch

---

[10]   Brené Brown, *The Gifts of Imperfection: Let go of who you think you're supposed to be and embrace who you are: Your guide to a wholehearted life,* Paperback edition. (Center City, Minnesota 55012: Hazelden Publishing and Educational Services, 2010), Page 25.

expectations often to fit in. It has taken me years to slowly take off layer after layer of masks I have put on to be the person who fits the mold (and I am sure I have even more masks to take off, with time). While they helped me get by at the time, they came with the harmful side effect of hiding my true self. These masks were my Joy Killers.

Some examples of my out-of-touch expectations for myself:

> Perfection (no mistakes allowed).
> Be exceptional in all categories and roles in my life.
> Be happy all the time.

Some examples of others' expectations of me:

> Be impressive.
> Be polite, and don't rock the boat.
> Follow the rules.

Let's identify some of the expectations you carry for yourself or from others. By doing so, we can become aware of what is driving you, then identify which expectations feel authentic to you and who you want to be.

Joy Killers Exercise:

Start by noticing expectations you have for yourself. Make a (nonjudgmental) list below:

_____

_____

_____

_____

_____

_____

_____

_____

_____

Now let's notice expectations others have for you (e.g., significant other, parents, kids, work, etc.):

_____

_____

_____

_____

_____

_____

_____

_____

_____

Review this list. Put a star next to expectations that feel authentic to you and an X next to expectations that do not feel authentic to you.

These answers make up your Joy Killer list, which are Soul Salary bills. In the budgeting step in the next section of the book, we will learn how to budget your Joy Killer bills to start peeling away your disguises and masks. You will learn to redefine expectations for yourself and release expectations that aren't aligned to make more room for joy. But first, we will dive into more bills—this next category I call Soul Suckers.

CHAPTER 10

Soul Suckers

Am I worthy?
If I get it all done
If I am productive
If I exceed all expectations
If I keep doing the hustle, the grind
If I work long hours
If I parent like I don't work
And work like I am not a parent
If I do, do, do to exhaustion
If I over-give, overdo it, overwhelm, over-everything?

Am I worthy?
And is it worth it
To try to be enough
To subscribe to Mom Martyr culture
To see who can be the most tired and worn out
To be afraid to make a mistake
To hold on to control
To not be able to relax?

These thoughts are an example of a common "Soul Sucker" bill—tying self-worth and enough-ness (feeling self-love and acceptance) to productivity. This chapter is about defining and identifying your Soul Suckers (i.e., fears and limiting beliefs) which keep you from fulfillment and achieving your legacy.

For example, in the string of thoughts above, I showcased my fear around my worthiness. I had tied my self-worth to my productivity and how much I can get done. I had a deep fear of being unlovable, not enough, and unworthy. My limiting belief associated with the above is all about the hustle, the grind, and worn-out mom culture (that you are only worthy as a mother and as a person if you are doing it all). If you aren't exhausted, are you even trying hard enough?

If you are in a similar thought spiral, don't worry—we are going to learn how to mitigate Soul Suckers like this. We will start by addressing both fear and limiting beliefs.

Let's start with fear. Fear does not allow us to act from a place of love. Fear stifles love in favor of primal survival responses. When there is a fear-inducing threat revealed to the brain, it signals a fight, flight, freeze, or fawn response. Below are some common fear triggers.

> Imagined events (e.g., thinking of scenarios that can go wrong when you travel with kids for the first time).
> Echoes of traumatic experiences (e.g., a mental health episode).
> Particular things or situations (e.g., phobias like heights, snakes).
> True dangers (e.g., being robbed).
> The unknown (e.g., taking on a new role, creating imposter syndrome and self-doubt).

> Future events (e.g., not taking the leap because of fear of failure/mistakes).

In Chapter 12, we will talk about ways to overcome fear and complete the stress cycle to get out of fear's fight, flight, freeze, or fawn responses. Addressing your fear helps you make decisions by following your heart, not your fears.

The other big Soul Suckers are limiting beliefs. As author Tony Robbins says, "Limiting beliefs are the stories we tell ourselves about who we are that hold us back from becoming who we are meant to be."[11] As the phrase suggests, these are beliefs that limit you in some way. They can even be used by your brain to avoid discomfort and the unknown.

Below are some common limiting beliefs statements:
> I do/don't.
  + I don't have enough experience.
  + I don't have what it takes.
  + I don't have time.
  + I don't deserve love.
  + I will do it myself.
  + I don't want to disappoint my parents, partner, or boss.
> I can/can't.
  + I can do it myself.
  + I can't do it; I have responsibilities.
  + I can't trust myself.
> I should/shouldn't/have to.
  + I have to keep them happy.
  + I have to be perfect.

---

[11] 1 Tony Robbins, "The complete guide to limiting beliefs," Tony Robbins, Accessed January 17, 2023, https://www.tonyrobbins.com/limiting-beliefs-guide.

> - ✦ I should go; it is expected of me.
> - ✦ I shouldn't go on that retreat; the kids need me.
- > I am/am not.
>   - ✦ I am not enough (good enough, smart enough, pretty enough).
>   - ✦ I am afraid.
>   - ✦ I am bad at _____.
>   - ✦ I am too old or too young.
- > Others are/will.
>   - ✦ No one will like me.
>   - ✦ People are cruel.
>   - ✦ People will think I am weird.
- > The world is/isn't.
>   - ✦ The world isn't safe.
>   - ✦ The world is full of hate.
>   - ✦ It's a man's world out there.
- > Life is/isn't.
>   - ✦ Life isn't fair.
>   - ✦ True love is made up.

These thoughts lead us to stay stuck, to overthink, to become overwhelmed, etc. Limiting beliefs often stifle our ability to grow into our true selves, achieve, take risks, or take new paths.

Think of your mind and your beliefs as a sculpture that is always in progress. In the early years, your parents, family, teachers, mentors, religion, education, life experiences, and how you were raised all started your piece of art for you. They picked the clay and began to shape the clay and the textures of the sculpture that is your mind and beliefs. As you grow, your personal piece of art becomes yours alone to modify, remove, add, and ultimately create. We become the creator, the attributed artist. We need to assess our artwork and decide which shapes and textures to keep in the sculpture, what new clay or pieces to bring in or add, what parts of the artwork to scrap and start over or alter to fit our vision for the sculpture of our minds. You get to decide who contributes to your artwork and what is added to or subtracted from the artwork, as you are an ever-changing and always-in-process piece of art and you have creative control! So, yes—you have limiting beliefs, but you can change your beliefs at any time to serve who you are becoming and want to be (albeit, this is easier said than done!).

In the next chapters, we will talk in detail about budgeting our bills. In Chapter 12, we will specifically budget Soul Suckers. Then, we will work on redefining your limiting beliefs to be beliefs that work for you and feel authentic and helpful. To work with Soul Suckers, however, we first must identify our fears and limiting beliefs before we can reframe and move forward.

Let's identify your Soul Suckers. Some of my Soul Suckers I found along the journey are listed below to help you ideate.

> Tying my worth to external validation.
> Fear of not being a good enough mom, especially if I don't "do it all."
> Scarcity limiting beliefs (e.g., I can't make money doing what I love).
> Parenting limiting beliefs (e.g., Kids need to obey and listen and behave; if they don't, I'm a bad parent).
> Fear of failure or mistakes and intense self-criticism when a mistake was made.
> I need to be independent, and asking for help is a failure.

Soul Suckers Exercise:

Create your Soul Sucker list by defining the obstacles between you and your fulfillment and legacy.

> What is causing the gap from where you are today to meeting your legacy statement from Chapter 5?

_____

_____

_____

_____

_____

_____

> What is getting in your way and stopping you from feeling fulfilled?

_____

_____

_____

_____

_____

> What are your fears? (See previous list of common fear triggers.)

_____

_____

_____

_____

_____

_____

_____

_____

_____

> ❯ What are your limiting beliefs? (See previous list of common ones.)

_____

_____

_____

_____

_____

_____

_____

_____

_____

> ❯ What are you *not* proud of?

_____

_____

_____

_____

_____

This Soul Suckers list outlines the rest of your Soul Salary bills.

Compare this list with your Joy Killers list, and any common themes between the two are your biggest Soul Salary bills.

If you're feeling discouraged by all these bills, just hold on tight. In the next chapters, we talk about how to reduce these Joy Killer and Soul Sucker bills.

Step 4
Budgeting and Budget Cuts

CHAPTER 11

Toodles, Joy Killers

School pictures are always posed. The kids are pretending to smile and hold themselves a certain way as orchestrated by the school photographer. Their smiles never look real, do they? So, my husband and I started a new tradition with our kids. On picture day, we not only rely on the school photographer for pictures, but we also take our own pictures of the boys before school, individually, in whatever pose they want. Such a big difference—in one, they are prim and proper and faking a smile (school pictures), and in the other, they are making goofy faces with their arms wide open (unscripted pictures). Masks and disguises can be sneaky.

Masks, disguises, illusions—we all master the art of disguise at some point in our lives to fit in. We make ourselves into something that is not authentic to our uniqueness to be accepted by our surrounding environment and culture. It can feel like Halloween every day. Will you keep choosing the mask?

After I first watched Disney's *Frozen* (2013), I sang Elsa's song, "Let it go," at the top of my lungs the whole ride home. The lyrics resonated, and the song felt good to belt out—singing like I used to as a kid, with no self-consciousness. Look for these moments that resonate with you (a quote, a song, something a person said to you in conversation, a recurring number or animal sign you keep seeing). These are little breadcrumbs on the journey, leading you back home to yourself.

In this chapter, we focus on letting go of Joy Killers (i.e., inauthentic expectations) by learning how to show off our light and beauty. Your true colors are hidden behind the disguises, poses, and masks—it's time to let them out! In this chapter, I urge you to do as the saying goes: "Be yourself. Everyone else is taken." Or as I like to remind myself: "Be you, unapologetically."

You can move away from focusing on meeting all the expectations by setting clear boundaries, identifying what you are in control of (and what you are not in control of), and setting personal intentions versus trying to meet society's, work's, and others' expectations—and your own inauthentic expectations.

Let's start with boundaries and control.

Boundaries and Control

According to the Merriam-Webster dictionary, a boundary is "something that indicates or fixes a limit or extent."[12] "Boundaries" has been a buzzword for a while now, but to put it plainly, you teach people how to treat you and you get what you expect. Some examples of boundaries include:

> ➤ Family boundary: The TV stays off during dinner.

---

[12] Merriam-Webster, "Boundary Definition and Meaning," Merriam-Webster, Accessed January 17, 2023, https://www.merriam-webster.com/dictionary/boundary.

> Work boundary: I don't work weekends.
> Personal boundary: I don't tolerate others yelling at me. I walk away from the situation.

I have found the key with boundaries is to focus on what you can control—which is a lot more than you likely realize. You are *always* in control of:

> Your actions (e.g., honesty with others, work ethic, integrity)
> Your reactions (e.g., body language, tone of voice)
> Your physical, mental, and emotional well-being (e.g., breath, self-talk, beliefs, physical fitness, diet, sleep)—of course excluding diagnoses or uncontrollable circumstances that affect these areas (e.g., insomnia, depression, stroke, cancer, etc.)

The first step in boundary work is to practice not breaking promises to yourself. Show yourself that you are trustworthy and respect your boundaries with yourself. If you promise yourself you are going to exercise thirty minutes per day, do it! If you are doing dry January (no alcohol), do it! Make sure your promises to yourself are achievable, meaningful to you, and in your control (e.g., promising yourself you will get a work promotion by a certain date is out of your control if you aren't self-employed).

Next, give yourself what you desire and need. You are able to meet almost all of your needs and desires. Yes, sometimes to meet those needs you do need help, but most of it you can give to yourself. Give yourself rest, buy yourself the chocolate, give yourself unconditional love, find support, and onward until your desires and needs are satisfied.

You have the control to improve your self-love, improve your self-awareness, and heal your trauma. We talk a lot about this in the next chapter on budgeting Soul Suckers, so for now, let's focus on what you can control about relationships with others—family, friends, coworkers, bosses, or strangers. A key grounding point before we start: Rarely can something steal your joy unless you allow it.

As author Dan Harris said, "There is no point in being unhappy about things you can't change, and no point being unhappy about things you can."[13] Now, we all know that we cannot control others, but you do get to decide what you allow and what you do not. You have three choices when it comes to boundaries crossed by others: you can let it go, address it, or store it. Storing the issues is not recommended, because the stress of your boundary being crossed doesn't just go away. It shows up in your health (mental, emotional, physical, or otherwise). There is a yoga saying, "Your issues are in your tissues." Since you have control over your issues, please don't store it in your body! I suggest using the "let it go" or "address it" methods instead. These options are both healthy ways to deal with others, and you get to choose which route to take. My rule of thumb is to choose to address it for relationships you wish to put energy into and improve; otherwise, choose to let it go.

---

[13]   Dan Harris, 10% Happier: How I tamed the voice in my head, reduced stress without losing my edge, and found self-help that actually works - a true story, Digital 5th Anniversary Edition. (Harper Collins Publishers, 2019). Loc 3414.

Expectations and Boundary Editing Exercise:

Edit the expectations you listed in the Joy Killer chapter (Chapter 9) to be only ones that feel authentic and aligned with who you want to be. Reframe them here to be healthy self-expectations.

_____

_____

_____

_____

_____

_____

_____

_____

_____

Where do you need to add boundaries to expectations others have of you or your own out-of-touch expectations?

_____

_____

_____

_____

_____

_____

Here is an example:

> Outside expectation: Be impressive.
> Healthy reframe: Be someone _I am_ proud of.
> Related boundary: I don't keep people in my life who I can't be authentically me around, or who try to mold me into something I am not.

Next, we will dive deeper into expectations and learn the difference between intention and expectation.

Intention versus Expectation

In Chapter 9, we talked about Joy Killers beginning with other people's expectations that we take on and our own out-of-touch expectations for ourselves. We alter this by setting intentions as often as possible versus having expectations. You will say goodbye to these Joy Killers by showing radical self-love, believing in your self-worth, and living in your power with self-confidence. Remember, you are worthy and enough as you are today.

I heard sociologist Martha Beck on Glennon Doyle's *We Can do Hard Things* podcast say, "Don't get consensus; come to your senses." What a profound concept and truth. We are taught to try to get the consensus of society, those around us, what is socially acceptable, what is okay, what is the best choice, etc., but the answer can only come from ourselves. Trust your senses, your intuition, and your gut. Ask your body—it never lies. Does it feel expansive, light, warm, cozy, exciting, and right? If so, this is a sign your body is saying yes. Also, notice when your body is saying no—in these cases, it may feel constrictive, heavy, panicky, fearful, and all wrong. Everyone is different in what they feel is a yes and a no in their body—start listening to yours. As a play on "follow your gut," my friend Brittney always says, "I just follow my belly button."

When I was a senior in college, I had two job offers I was torn between. One was for Company A that I had interned with for three summers. Their headquarters was located near my hometown. It was known, comfortable, and made logical

98

sense to take this offer. The other option was for another great company, Company B. I hadn't worked there before, and it was likely if I took that job that I would need to move away from my boyfriend and family to live alone in another state. Logically it made no sense, but my heart was calling me to pick this unknown choice. I had majorly connected with the campus interview team and felt that they were my people. My body, mind, and soul wanted to say yes and do this, but it was based purely on intuition without a logical explanation. And having a strong logical mind, I had a deep need for the decision to make factual sense. I called friends and relatives to help me make the decision.

I was trying to get consensus/permission from those around me to avoid making this hard choice by myself. I even made a list of pros and cons, and no matter how I worked it, the logical solution, the company I had interned with for three summers, won the game. It wasn't sitting right with me to pick the safe option because I really wanted to go with Company B.

I stepped back and looked at it from a broader perspective. What was my intention with this decision? I determined that my intention was to follow my intuition even if it was the scarier path. So, in a major act of rebellious self-love, I picked the scary, nonlogical route and went with the unknown.

I ended up spending thirteen years with that company, and it was one of the best decisions I made. My husband (boyfriend at the time) followed me to California and found a different career path that he continues to excel in. My move out of state brought my now husband and me closer and led to a wonderful marriage to my best friend and partner in life. We had our two kiddos while I worked at this company. I grew up and had huge life events with this company. Reflecting back, I am so proud of that decision years ago while listening to my gut and my intentions. I chose to go against reason and listen to myself and what I wanted (not what others wanted for me), not knowing if it would work out or not. I took the leap and chose intentions over expectations, and I was rewarded one hundredfold.

Are you willing to leap?

Let's look at your intentions versus expectations by starting with some definitions.

Intention—so much power in a single word. According to Collins Dictionary, it is "an idea or plan of what you are going to do."[14]

Expectations—so much heaviness in a single word. According to Collins Dictionary, they are "strong beliefs someone has about the proper way someone should behave or something should happen."[15]

Are you going to drink from the fire hose and try to meet all expectations, or are you going to be intentional about what you do and don't do? About what you want and don't want?

Here is an example. Let's say your broad intention is "I want ease in my life."

Specific intention: I am going to allow hosting Thanksgiving to be easy.

[14] Collins, "Definition of Intention," Collins Dictionary, Accessed January 17, 2023, https://www.collinsdictionary.com/us/dictionary/english/intention.

[15] Collins, "Definition of Expectation," Collins Dictionary, Accessed January 17, 20230, https://www.collinsdictionary.com/us/dictionary/english/expectation.

Actions aligned with your intention:

> I am going to order a Thanksgiving dinner kit or premade turkey from the grocery store.
> I am going to ask everyone to bring a dish to Thanksgiving.

Action aligned with expectations and out of alignment with your intention:

> I am going to impress my whole family and in-laws by making the perfect turkey, sides, and dessert.
> I am going to cook in the kitchen for days preparing for this meal.

So, are you going to be intentional or let expectations run your life? The choice is yours and in your control.

Let's practice this by setting the intention for the day and week (you can do them for any period of time, but let's start here for now). Intentions are meant to support you and help you filter out and deprioritize tasks that do not align with your main intentions. After you write your intention, look at your to-do list for the day or week and list the top three critical tasks that need to be done for each. If you are having trouble setting an intention, reflect on your legacy statement and write down more short-term intentions that align with that.

Some examples of daily intentions:

> I need time for me—my intention is to do three things for myself today.
> I have a big deadline at work—my intention this week is to meet this deadline by breaking it out into

manageable chunks. I will also make it easier to take care of my basic needs by ordering takeout for dinners.

> I need to set myself up for the week—my intention today is to do laundry and meal planning.

> I have a work trip coming up—my intention this week is to prepare and pack for the work trip.

Let's aim for progress, not perfection, and to keep it simple. Remember, life is an experiment, and you are allowed to have failed experiments, then debrief and try again with a modified experiment. You have not failed unless you stop trying!

Intention Exercise:

> What is your intention for today?

_____

_____

> What are your top three critical tasks for today?

1. Priority #1

_____

_____

2. Priority #2

_____

_____

3. Priority #3

_____

_____

➤ Do they align with your intention? If not, how can you alter them to align?

_____

_____

_____

_____

➤ What is your intention for the week?

_____

_____

➤ What are your top three critical tasks for this week?

1. Priority #1

_____

_____

2. Priority #2

_____

_____

3. Priority #3

_____

_____

➤ Do they align with your intention? If not, how can you alter them to align?

_____

_____

_____

_____

> ❯ Reflections?

_____

_____

_____

_____

> ❯ How did the exercise feel?

_____

_____

_____

Did you feel some lightness as you lowered your expectations? Did you feel some clarity as you set intentions? Or did you feel overwhelmed by how many boundaries you needed to set to reduce the expectations placed on you?

However you felt, you should be proud of yourself for doing the work. This is really hard stuff! I have found that the Soul Salary bills (including Joy Killers) are the hardest to reduce, but some of the most rewarding changes to make on the journey toward more joy and fulfillment.

✦ ✦ ✦ ✦ ✦

CHAPTER 12

So Long, Soul Suckers

When I had my first child, I was battling postpartum depression and anxiety, all while coming back to work to a new role, a new boss, and to support the recent announcement of the closure of the manufacturing plant I worked at. I was to be in charge of climate and culture to support the plant employees in this transition, *while* I was going through a major transition myself. I was lucky because the company I worked for offered a program to help cope with all the changes, including therapy. I decided to use this benefit, and for the first time ever, I went into therapy.

It was incredibly helpful to move out of several stress cycles and talk out my feelings with an unbiased professional. I shared my success with a few people I worked with, and a few of them also sought support. Therapy and mental health can be viewed as such a taboo topic, but it shouldn't be. It can be life changing and incredibly effective. No one should have to keep mental health issues to themselves out of shame or fear. Mental health is just as valid as physical health. I still have a wonderful therapist that I see as needed for a mental health tune-up.

This isn't an advertisement for therapy (although it is starting to sound like one!) but a call to action for you to do what is needed to cope with fear, limiting beliefs, or other unresolved things within you and to complete the stress cycle they trigger. If you need support, know it is strong as hell for a person to realize they need help, ask for it, and get it, in whatever format they choose.

Soul Suckers are the fears and limiting beliefs holding us back from living our soul purpose and creating our legacy. Let's say "so long" to these time and energy suckers!

Fear

We will start by addressing fear. We talked in Chapter 10 about fear being related to survival instincts and perceived threats. Fear's purpose is to keep you safe, so the goal is not to eliminate all fear—but we can become overactive or stuck in fear. When this happens, we cannot complete the stress cycle and move out of our flight, flight, freeze, or fawn state. When we don't complete the cycle, we don't get back to feeling calm or safe, or recover and rest.

Let's look at each of the four F responses, one at a time. Fight response is the urge to go head-to-head with the threat (including behaviors such as aggression, anger, yelling). Flight response is the urge to run from the threat (including behaviors such as avoidance and numbing with substances). Freeze is the body's urge to protect itself from the threat by not moving (including behaviors such as shutting down and being silent). Fawn is the urge to try to please to avoid the threat (including behaviors such as people-pleasing or being overly helpful). Other experiences associated with fear include anxiety, panic attacks, PTSD, and more.

Fear has many key physical effects as well, like increased heart rate, faster breathing, sweating, chills, digestive changes, etc. Some fears are based on survival instincts, while others are learned and/or are connected to traumatic experiences. There is a broad range of trauma experiences, from being bullied to life-threatening experiences and everything in between and beyond.

Again, we are not trying to get rid of all fear, as the instinctual part does work to keep you safe. But if you are stuck in the fear stress cycle (fight, flight, freeze, fawn), it is time to work through those cycles to get back to calm and rest. You need to be able to listen with your heart and gut versus reacting to trigger responses of fear and stress.

Fears you cannot control are things like other people's reactions or opinions (e.g., what if she thinks poorly of me?), uncontrollable circumstances (e.g., getting laid off from work), etc.

Fears that you have some control over are opportunities for proactive work to address them. You can control things that involve your actions (e.g., you are afraid you will always be exhausted, so you take a vacation, ask for/hire help, remove things from your plate, etc.), the parts of well-being you can control (e.g., you are afraid you are going to get sick, so you start taking vitamins, go to regular doctor visits, etc.), your reactions (e.g., you are worried you will get uncontrollably angry at your rude aunt, so you start meditation and other calming techniques to control your anger), etc.

As you can see, fears you have some control over have proactive actions you can take. You can mitigate, support yourself through them, and/or eliminate each fear.

For example, if the fear is "I am scared of getting sick," a few actions could be:

> I will use hand sanitizer after being in public places. (Mitigate.)
> I will talk to a therapist about coping techniques for anxiety around getting sick. (Support.)
> I will isolate at home during flu season. (Eliminate.)

Let's write about your fears and put this into practice.

Fear Defeated, Joy Greeted Exercise:

> Journal your fears: Review the fears you wrote in Chapter 10 and empty out all of the thoughts related to those fears. Write it all out—yes, everything! Don't put your pen down!

_____

_____

_____

_____

_____

_____

_____

_____

_____

_____

_____

_____

_____

_____

> ❯ Focus on what you can control.
>   ✦ Read the journaling of your fears and cross out what you *cannot* control.
>   ✦ Read through what you just crossed out. I suggest closing your eyes and taking three deep breaths. As you exhale, loudly and aggressively sigh out your breath as you physically let go of those items you cannot control.
> ❯ Make action plans for what you *can* control.
>   ✦ Read the remaining fears and rank them from first to last in terms of power the fear has over you right now.
>   ✦ Use this list to write out actions you could take to mitigate them, support yourself through them, and/or eliminate each fear for the top three fears.

Fear 1

_____

_____

_____

_____

_____

Fear 2

_____

_____

_____

_____

Fear 3

_____

_____

_____

_____

> Prioritize.
  - Read this list of actions and number each one 1, 2, or 3 based on how big of an impact that action would have on addressing your fear, 1 being a big impact and 3 being a small impact.
> Do it!
  - Take action starting with the big-impact items ranked 1 and working down the list. Each step you take brings you closer and closer to joy and fulfillment. Which action will you start with?

_____

_____

_____

_____

After you've addressed the fears themselves as best as you can, it is time to try to trigger the "rest" cycle by ending the "stress" cycle. Examples of common ways people complete the stress cycle to move out of fear include:

> Movement/exercise
> Sleep
> Mental breaks (e.g., screen-free time, meditation or quiet time, no inputs, breathing exercises)
> Connection (e.g., people, animals, outdoors, hugs, kisses, laughter)
> Creativity (e.g., writing, dancing, art)
> Getting support (e.g., ask your partner, friends, or family to support you, hire help or trade services for help)
> Imagination (e.g., reading a book, watching a movie)
> Letting it out (e.g., cry it out, talk it out, shout it out, sing it out, literally scream it out)

Sarah Harmon, a mental health therapist, once organized a group of women to meet up in a field and literally scream out their rage, frustration, and anger to release emotions, a process backed by science. It worked so well, some moms continued this screaming work in small groups or alone. I am just saying—it is an option.[16]

Another philosophy is to deal with things as they happen instead of worrying about what could happen. This more laid-back demeanor also reminds me of the quote by Roman philosopher Seneca: "We suffer more in our imagination than in reality."[17] The goal is to be present in reality right now as much as possible, not what could happen in the future or what has happened in the past. Trust you can handle whatever comes your way. In the wise words of Dory from *Finding Nemo*— "Just keep swimming!"

Limiting Beliefs

Now let's talk about those pesky limiting beliefs. In Chapter 10, you identified your limiting beliefs, and that is the first step! Now let's review that list and redefine and edit those limiting beliefs so that they work for you, feel more authentic to the

---

[16] Tony Hicks, "The COVID-19 Pandemic Can Make You Want to Scream... and That Could Be Helpful," Healthline, Accessed on January 20, 2023, https://www.healthline.com/health-news/the-covid-19-pandemic-can-make-you-want-to-scream-and-that-could-be-helpful.

[17] Lucius Annaeus Seneca, "On groundless fears," Moral letters to Lucilius, Letter 13.

true you, and feel positive and uplifting instead of restrictive. A key point in the new belief is that it must feel believable to you.

Here are a few of my reframes of my limiting beliefs:

Old belief: I need to be in control.
New belief: I surrender control to tasks that I delegate.

Old belief: I should _____ (enter anything here).
New belief: Should isn't a good enough reason to do something.

Old belief: Kids should behave and listen to what I ask every time.
New belief: Kids are not soldiers; their thoughts, needs, and feelings are valid and worth taking time to listen to.

Redefining Limiting Beliefs Exercise:

Do this with at least the top five limiting beliefs from the Chapter 10 exercise that feel the most restrictive to you today. Make sure the redefined belief feels authentic and believable to you.

Old belief: _____

_____

New redefined belief: _____

_____

Old belief: _____

_____

New redefined belief: _____

_____

Old belief: _____

_____

New redefined belief: _____

_____

Old belief: _____

_____

New redefined belief: _____

_____

Old belief: _____

_____

New redefined belief: _____

_____

Another way to create more authentic and inspiring beliefs is to use affirmations, positive things you can say to yourself that are true now, or will be true to the person who you strive to be in the future, written as if they are already true (like a Jedi mind trick!). Here are some more common examples you can use:

> I am loved.
> I express myself.
> I am strong.
> I am creative.
> I am safe.
> I care for myself.
> I accept myself.
> I speak my truth.
> I trust myself.
> I know myself.

If you need some more examples, here are a few of my own I used throughout the journey:

> I work from the heart.
> I am free.
> I go with the flow.
> I choose ease.
> I am strong and courageous.

You could choose a powerful one (e.g., I love you, queen), a sweet one (e.g., I love you unconditionally), or a motivational one (e.g., Girl, treat yourself; you made it through another day). Whatever feels authentic and uplifting to you!

Affirmations Exercise:

Write out some affirmations that make you feel positive and uplifted. Write them as if they are already true.

_____

_____

_____

_____

_____

_____

_____

As you use your affirmations, ask yourself if you are speaking to yourself like someone you love.

Do you typically use words you are proud of when you talk to yourself or when you talk about yourself?

Catch yourself when you are talking unkindly to yourself and tell your brain to stop talking about your friend (i.e., you) like that. Be the mediator and shift thoughts to more loving words, like the new beliefs you have come up with in the workbook, to free yourself from old beliefs holding you back from achieving your ideal life. Remember to realize that you had a negative thought and come up with a replacement thought that is kinder and more authentic to you. For example, I could have a negative thought like, *I will never last as an entrepreneur*, notice it, and replace it with *I am learning how to be an entrepreneur and give myself grace to make mistakes*. My husband, Henry, calls negative self-talk "head trash." So, take out the trash!

My challenge for you today is to show yourself some love with the support you documented for relieving fears, by using your redefined limiting beliefs, and by saying your affirmations. You can also post these somewhere you will see them consistently to remind you not to let the Soul Suckers win!

Now that we have talked about how to budget those Joy Killers and Soul Suckers, it is time for some budget cuts!

CHAPTER 13

Budget Cuts

There are always more than just black and white options—you just need to be willing to get creative with your solutions and mix some colors!

This works for solutions to problems and also for the beliefs we hold. It does not have to be so extreme as only two choices. Be open to creative solutions. My theory is you have at least four paths when it comes to reducing and cutting bills:

1. Eliminate
2. Delegate
3. Reduce
4. Add fun to

I know the delegate step has some people feeling uncomfortable. They say it takes a village, but we are also taught to be independent and strong above all. Here's the secret: you can be independent and strong *and* get yourself a tribe, a sisterhood, a brotherhood, a village, a posse, a squad, to support you! For every day, but especially when you need to cocoon and refresh, relax, and heal. Allow yourself to get help and support. Allow others to have a role in your life. Your true soul tribe is eager to support you and honored you want them as part of your squad. As my good friend Jim says, "No one walks alone." The true joy in life comes from the moment that you allow the village to help. Once you realize that life is not meant to be done alone and you embrace it, life becomes a lot easier—and more fun.

Here is an example of all four options and how they work. Do you know about the elf-on-the-shelf Christmas tradition? If you don't know of it, I am so jealous! It is a little elf doll that comes to watch the kids to make sure they are good and reports back to Santa each December night leading up to Christmas. The elf "moves" each night, and in the morning, the kids wake up and try to find his new perch in the house. I see other moms dress up the elf and put it in Pinterest-worthy scenarios (the elf wants to bake Christmas cookies with you or the elf caused mischief by spilling some candy). Doing the elf-on-the-shelf tradition as part of the holidays does *not* bring me joy and, in fact, stresses me out. I always have to remember to move him, and it makes me feel guilty for not having cool scenes and outfits with the elf set up each night. It is now a tradition that my kids look forward to and I do not; however, we always have choices on how to move forward. So, let's use the above options for what next steps could be:

① Eliminate: Stop the tradition. Our elf (who we named Alfie) went back to the North Pole to help Santa. Alfie moved on to a new family this year. Alfie is now with your younger cousins.

② Delegate: Ask my husband to take point on the Alfie responsibilities.

③ Reduce: Have the elf move less frequently than daily. During the COVID pandemic, I heard of parents that put the elf in a fourteen-day quarantine to avoid moving it each night (these are my people!). Or you could bring the elf out December 15th instead of starting December 1st—Alfie was delayed because of a winter storm in the North Pole!

④ Add fun to it: Find a mom friend to share the ideas of what to do with Alfie or have a competition with a mom friend on who can do the laziest scenes with the elf.

Spoiler alert—this is a true story, and I ended up delegating. My husband took over elf responsibilities, and turns out he actually really enjoys it!

Budget Cuts Exercise:

Pick one Joy Killer and one Soul Sucker to do budget cuts on from your lists in Chapters 9 and 10, then write out four options for each.

Joy Killer:

_____

_____

➤ Eliminate: _____

_____

➤ Delegate:_____

_____

➤ Reduce:_____

_____

➤ Add fun to: _____

_____

Soul Sucker:

_____

_____

> Eliminate:_____

_____

> Delegate:_____

_____

> Reduce:_____

_____

> Add fun to: _____

_____

Remember S.M.A.R.T. goals from Chapter 7 (specific, measurable, achievable, relevant, timely)? It's time to make some S.M.A.R.T. goals to reduce your bills and commit to doing some budget cuts. Here is an example of a S.M.A.R.T. goal for budgeting:

I will resign from the P.T.O. by the end of the month to free up time for the joy I find in game night with the kids.

Now let's break it down into the S.M.A.R.T. framework:

- ○ **Specific** goal: *I will resign from the P.T.O.*
- ○ How will it be **Measured** (how will you know you have been successful): *Resign.*
- ○ Is this goal **Achievable** (if not, break it into smaller steps) and how: *Achievable in one step of resigning.*

- ○ Is this goal **Relevant** to increasing your Soul Salary paychecks by raising your joy (joy list), fulfillment (legacy statement), and/or basic needs and nonnegotiables? *To free up time for the joy I find in game night with the kids.*
- ○ When will you reach this goal? Make it **Timely**: *By the end of the month.*

Budgeting S.M.A.R.T. Goal Exercise:

Set your first goal below.

➤ What is one thing you will do first to reduce your bills? Use the S.M.A.R.T (specific, measurable, achievable, relevant, timely) goal framework:

✦ Specific goal:

_____

_____

_____

✦ How will it be Measured (how will you know you have been successful):

_____

_____

✦ Is this goal Achievable (if not, break it into smaller steps) and how:

_____

_____

_____

_____

✦ Is this goal Relevant to reducing your Soul Salary bills by letting go of Joy Killers and Soul Suckers?

_____

_____

_____

✦ When will you reach this goal? Make it Timely:

_____

_____

❯ What help do you need to make this happen?
  ✦ Examples: Learning material (a book, course, teacher), support from others (family member, travel agent, therapist), time (vacation time, time without kids), money.

_____

_____

_____

_____

✦ Don't forget your nonnegotiables (i.e., boundaries) and the conversations or steps that need to happen here.

_____

_____

_____

_____

Pick one and then keep coming back to eliminate, delegate, reduce, add fun to your list to reduce your bills one at a time. I will say it again—progress, not perfection!

With these tools at your disposal, it's time to say,

> See ya,
> Good riddance,
> Advertersene,
> Sayonara,
> Adios,
> Bye bye,
>
> to your bills!

Bills are almost always the most impactful focus area when it comes to Soul Salary, so do the work—don't skip this part just because it feels heavy. Reduce those fears, reframe those limiting beliefs, shed expectations that are not authentic to you, and set those boundaries.

In the final chapter, we will talk about going beyond raising your Soul Salary and taking it up a notch. It's time to finally become a High Earner in Soul Salary and stay there!

Conclusion

✦ ✦ ✦ ✦ ✦

CHAPTER 14

Become a High Earner

I embrace each season by showing myself love and radical self-care (e.g., taking care of my needs before giving to others). In the metaphorical fall and winter season of life, I shed "leaves" (i.e., bills) of what no longer serves me to make room for new green leaves (i.e., paychecks) in the spring and summer seasons of life. When you are a High Earner in Soul Salary and find yourself worthy, you need to continue to challenge yourself to become the best you can be each season. Measure your life in seasons of self-love, over and over. Keep choosing this so you can have significant freedom to live in your joy and fulfillment.

Remember, Soul Salary is the value your soul receives when your time and energy are spent in alignment with your passions, your life purpose/mission on Earth, and what feeds your soul. A Soul Salary paycheck is the joy and fulfillment your soul desires. It is what fills you up. A Soul Salary bill is the Joy Killers and Soul Suckers that drain you. As CEO of your life, your job is to find what paychecks your soul desires and what bills you have, and then to increase the paychecks (give yourself raises and promotions) and decrease the bills (say, toodles, Joy Killers, and see ya, Soul Suckers, and implement budget cuts).

Keep doing this cycle until you become a High Earner in Soul Salary. You'll know you've made it when your soul feels warm, joyful, lit up, passionate, useful, happy, and fulfilled a majority of the time.

When you have reached Soul Salary High Earner status, congratulations!

Unfortunately, the honor is not guaranteed to continue forever and ever without some continued work on your end. As Greek philosopher, Heraclitus, famously said, "Change is the only constant in life."[18] That is why I encourage you to do some continued education, recertify yourself as a High Earner, give yourself an annual performance review, and keep growing and flowing with the changes in your life.

An excellent way to check in with your soul is to periodically redo the Soul Salary assessment on what your Soul Salary is. Why don't you retake it now to see how far you've come since beginning this book? You can find it in Chapter 2 or at www.JessKaskov.com/SoulSalary.

As a reminder, if your results are low in joy, see Chapters 4 and 9. If your results are low in fulfillment, see Chapters 5 and 10. If your results are low in basic needs, see Chapter 3. I have created a workbook at the end of this chapter that includes all the exercises you did in the previous chapters so you have a place to do the work again when you feel called to make some edits in your Soul Salary.

---

[18] Jorge Tendeiro, "Heraclitus: The only constant is change," Socratic Life, Accessed on January 20, 2023, https://socraticlife. com.au/heraclitus-the-only-constant-is-change/.

Don't go back to cruise control! You are the driver, the CEO, and you are free! Check in with yourself and continue to prioritize your soul.

Profound Impact on the World

I have always believed in this African proverb (quoted by the Dalai Lama): "If you think you are too small to make a difference, you haven't spent the night with a mosquito." Each person who works on spreading love and joy to themselves makes a difference in the world. When you elevate your vibration to one of love and joy, you elevate your surroundings.

I remember a story from the "Transcendental Meditation: Benefit, News & More" web page that associated large groups practicing meditation with significant reductions in U.S. homicide and urban violent crime rates during an intervention period of three years. In fact, when just 1 percent of a community practiced meditation, the crime rate was reduced by 16 percent on average. This effect has been coined the Maharishi effect, and I believe it helps prove my point that you are never too small to make a difference in your life, your community, the world, the universe, and beyond.[19]

I am hopeful that this book—born of my journey to bring love, joy, and fulfillment to myself—has helped spread joy to you, and that you will spread it to others just by taking the journey yourself. I hope this book has a similar Maharishi-type effect because the biggest impact you can make in this world is

---

[19]   Mary Swift, "Study on the Maharishi Effect: Can group meditation lower crime rate and violence?", Transcendental Meditation: Benefits, News, & More, Accessed January 17, 2023. https://tmhome. com/study-maharishi-effect-group-meditation-crime-rate/.

to spread love and joy broadly, starting with yourself. The goal of life is to feel as much joy and fulfillment as possible, which means to have as high a Soul Salary as possible.

Let's change the world—starting with you!

Warmly,
Jess

Soul Salary Workbook

Soul Salary Basics:

CHAPTER 1

What Do You Do?

Fill these in (pick at least seven things you are or aspire to be):

I am _____.

I am _____.

I am _____.

I am _____.

I am _____.

I am _____.

I am _____.

CHAPTER 2

What is *Your* Soul Salary?

Soul Salary Baseline Exercise:

Think about your typical day. How much of your waking time and energy are spent on items that feel joyful and fulfilling? Would you say it is 99 percent? Forty percent? Twenty-five? Two?

Write your answers below for a baseline.

> Where do you think you fall in Soul Salary today?

_____

> How much of your waking time and energy are spent on things that make you feel joyous and fulfilled?

_____

Your Soul Salary Assessment:

Answer each question below as a yes or no. Pick the answer that comes to mind first so you don't overthink it! (also available at www.JessKaskov.com/SoulSalary)

1. Are you taking care of your physical needs (diet, exercise, sleep)? Yes No
2. Are you taking care of your mental and emotional needs? Yes No
3. Do you trust yourself? Yes No
4. Are you content even if you haven't been doing the productive "grind" or "hustling"? Yes No
5. Do you make time for rest and free time? Yes No
6. Do you have plenty of energy for the day? Yes No
7. Are you fulfilled in your life right now? Yes No
8. Do you feel fulfilled in your relationships? Yes No
9. Are you fulfilled in your career? Yes No
10. Are you proud of your life right now? Yes No
11. Are you proud of who you are right now? Yes No
12. Do you feel like you are fulfilling your life purpose? Yes No
13. Do you feel joyful and happy in your life? Yes No
14. Is your life fun? Yes No
15. Do you feel free? Yes No
16. Do you feel lit up, passionate, and on fire? Yes No
17. Do you do what you want/desire to do? Yes No
18. Do you feel free to do what you want? Yes No

Let's score your responses. Tally up all of your "yes" responses for the eighteen questions and see where you fall below:

> Sixteen-plus "yes" responses:
  ✦ You are a High Earner! That means you are a person who is very aligned with their

joy and likely feel warm, lit up, passionate, useful, and fulfilled.

> Eleven to fifteen "yes" responses:
> > ✦ You are middle class. That means you are likely a person who is aware of what brings them joy and fulfillment but has not aligned their time and energy to maximize this.

> Ten or less "yes" responses:
> > ✦ You are considered at minimum wage. That means you are a person who likely does not know what brings them joy and fulfillment. You are not prioritizing yourself, your joy, your self-love, and/or your self-care.

The questions are also divided into three subcategories for you to assess some ingredients of your Soul Salary:

1. Basic Needs
2. Fulfillment
3. Joy

Total up all of your "yes" responses for questions 1 through 6. These are the Basic Needs questions. Examples in this category include meeting physical, emotional, and mental needs as well as trusting yourself. See below for how you rank in this subcategory.

> High Earner: six "yes" responses
> Middle Class: four to five "yes" responses
> Minimum Wage: three or less "yes" responses

Total up all of your "yes" responses for questions 7 through 12. These are the Fulfillment questions. Examples in this category include fulfillment in relationships, career, and life purpose, as well as pride in your life and who you are. See below for how you rank in this subcategory.

> High Earner: six "yes" responses
> Middle Class: four to five "yes" responses
> Minimum Wage: three or less "yes" responses

Total up all of your "yes" responses for questions 13 through 18. These are the Joy questions. Examples in this category include joy, happiness, fun, passion, freedom, and doing what you want/desire. See below for how you rank in this subcategory.

> High Earner: six "yes" responses
> Middle Class: four to five "yes" responses
> Minimum Wage: three or less "yes" responses

Reflections:

Sit with your results for a moment. Write out any feelings or thoughts that come up for you. This can be a hard moment as you see the numbers on paper, and I honor you for taking a moment to assess and get feedback on where in your life you could feel more joyful, loved, and whole. Remember that you can do the uncomfortable.

> What was your original guess of your Soul Salary?

_____

> ➤ Did your guess match or differ from your total Soul Salary score and your Basic Needs, Fulfillment, and Joy subcategory scores? If so, how?

_____

_____

_____

_____

> ➤ What resonates with you?

_____

_____

_____

_____

> ➤ What surprises you?

_____

_____

_____

_____

> ➤ Did this exercise bring up any emotions?

_____

_____

_____

_____

CHAPTER 3

Demand Minimum Wage—It's the Law

Pause and take inventory of your body. How do you feel in your body, mind, and emotions today?

> Body:

_____

_____

> Mind:

_____

_____

> Emotions:

_____

_____

What is a step you could take toward supporting your body, mind, and emotions today?

> Body:

_____

_____

_____

_____

> Mind:

_____

_____

_____

_____

> Emotions:

_____

_____

_____

_____

If you have capacity to go broader than little wins today, reflect on what has worked in the past to support your physical, mental, and emotional needs.

> Body:

_____

_____

_____

_____

_____

_____

> Mind:

_____

_____

_____

_____

_____

_____

> Emotions:

_____

_____

_____

_____

_____

_____

Which questions did you answer "no" to from the Basic Needs section of the Soul Salary assessment?

> Are you taking care of your physical needs (diet, exercise, sleep)?
> Are you taking care of your mental and emotional needs?
> Do you trust yourself?

> ➤ Are you content even if you haven't been doing the productive "grind" or "hustling"?
> ➤ Do you make time for rest and free time?
> ➤ Do you have plenty of energy for the day?

Reflections:

What is one question from this section that you primarily want to focus on to enhance your basic needs (the one that would make the biggest impact if worked on)?

_____

Why did you answer "no" to this question? What are the biggest gaps?

_____

_____

_____

_____

_____

Imagine you are completely fulfilled in this area—visualize it and feel it—and then write ideas to improve this area. Write down all your ideas, even if it includes taking three months of vacation to Fiji. Enjoy the ideation process, even including what you might think is infeasible.

_____

_____

_____

_____

_____

_____

_____

_____

_____

Pick one thing to do *this week* and then commit to the next thing and then the next until you are meeting your basic needs at a middle-class level or better!

_____

_____

Nonnegotiables Exercise:

Write out your nonnegotiables in life—the hard lines. Envision you are looking for your ideal life. What would be the nonnegotiables (whether they are being met currently or not)? Write them below:

My nonnegotiables are:

> Physical:

_____

_____

> **Mental:**

_____

_____

> **Emotional:**

_____

_____

> **Time:**

_____

_____

> **Energy:**

_____

_____

Step 1
Soul Salary Paychecks

CHAPTER 4

Where is Your Joy?

Joy Moments Exercise:

Spend at least fifteen minutes reminiscing through these questions to get the full effect:

> ➤ List moments in your life when you felt the happiest. Go beyond big life events like weddings and births. These can be moments with friends, family, by yourself, traveling, outdoors, indoors, at home, or at work.

_____

_____

_____

_____

_____

_____

_____

_____

_____

_____

> What about each memory made you so happy?

_____

_____

_____

_____

_____

_____

_____

> Think about the five senses in those moments. Was it the sound of waves, the smell of pie cooking, the taste of fresh-picked fruit, warmth of the sun on your skin, or the view at the top after a mountain hike?

_____

_____

_____

_____

_____

_____

_____

> Take yourself back to those moments and feel them. Feel the high-vibration energy and think about what you want to take from it going forward to recreate the happiness. Write them here.

_____

_____

_____

_____

_____

_____

_____

Joy Exercise:

> What brings you joy?

_____

_____

_____

_____

_____

_____

> What makes you feel joyful?

_____

_____

_____

_____

_____

> How do you find joy with each of these?
    ✦ Friends

    _____

    _____

    ✦ Family

    _____

    _____

    ✦ Alone time

    _____

    _____

    ✦ Self-care/pampering

    _____

    _____

    ✦ Work

    _____

    _____

✦ Personal time

_____

_____

✦ Media

_____

_____

✦ Your environment (indoor or outdoor)

_____

_____

✦ Hobbies and activities

_____

_____

❯ What makes you smile?

_____

_____

_____

_____

❯ What makes you laugh?

_____

_____

_____

_____

> ➤ What makes your heart sing?

_____

_____

_____

_____

> ➤ What feels like play?

_____

_____

_____

_____

Your Joy List Exercise:

Review your responses in the Joy and Moments exercises and write down the similarities and items you feel give you the most joy. This is your joy list!

_____

_____

_____

_____

_____

_____

_____

_____

_____

_____

✦ ✦ ✦ ✦ ✦

CHAPTER 5

What is Your Legacy?

Pride Moments Exercise:

> What are *you* most proud of in your life so far?

_____

_____

_____

_____

_____

_____

_____

_____

_____

_____

> ❯ List those moments in your life where you felt this pride. Go beyond big life events like weddings and births. These can be moments with friends, family, by yourself, traveling, outdoors, indoors, at home, or at work.

_____

_____

_____

_____

_____

_____

_____

> ❯ What about each memory made you feel so proud?

_____

_____

_____

_____

_____

_____

> Take yourself back to those moments and feel them. Feel the high-vibration energy and think about what you want to take from it going forward in your legacy. Write them here.

_____

_____

_____

_____

_____

_____

_____

Legacy Exercise:

What is your legacy? Answer these questions:

> What do you want to be remembered for?

_____

_____

_____

_____

_____

_____

_____

✦ Why?

_____

_____

> When you leave this life, what do you want to leave behind in terms of your legacy?

_____

_____

_____

_____

_____

✦ Why?

_____

_____

> What do you want other people to say about you at your funeral? If you could write your eulogy, what would you want to be in there?

_____

_____

_____

_____

_____

✦ Why?

_____

_____

> Why?

_____

_____

_____

> Why?

_____

_____

_____

> Why?

_____

_____

_____

Legacy Statement Exercise:

> Review your responses from the Pride Moments exercise and Legacy exercise and determine the similarities and items you feel most passionate about. What are they?

_____

_____

_____

_____

_____

_____

_____

_____

_____

> Create your legacy statement. Try many iterations until you get the one that resonates the most.

_____

_____

_____

_____

_____

_____

_____

Reflections:

Read through your responses to these exercises.

> Is there anything that surprises you?

_____

_____

_____

_____

> How do you feel reading through this list? Nostalgia, pride, contentment, drive to do more, disappointment? Notice your emotions. All are valid and allowed.

_____

_____

_____

_____

Note if there are common themes between the joy list and legacy statement. These themes are where you have the largest "income" potential in your Soul Salary paycheck.

_____

_____

_____

_____

_____

_____

CHAPTER 6

Your Ideal ~~Job~~ Life

Visualization Exercise:

Sit up in your chair and close your eyes. Take some deep breaths until you feel calm and grounded. Visualize that you have your ideal life. What does a perfect day look like to you? Sit with it for a few minutes and enjoy the sensory experience of living the life you desire. Take a final deep breath and open your eyes.

Write your reflections:

> I saw:

_____

> I heard:

_____

> I smelled:

_____

> ➤ I tasted:

_____

> ➤ I felt:

_____

Job Requirements Exercise:

What would you need to do to meet the job requirements/
prerequisites to live 100 percent in this ideal ~~job~~ life?

_____

_____

_____

_____

_____

_____

_____

_____

_____

_____

Step 2
Raises and Promotions

CHAPTER 7

Give Yourself a Raise!

Raise Brainstorm Exercise:

Let's start brainstorming how you can raise your Soul Salary.
Answer these questions:

> What is the most significant thing you could do for
  your soul?

_____

_____

_____

_____

_____

> What is the best thing that can happen for you?

_____

_____

_____

_____

_____

> What are some things you could do to advance your life?

_____

_____

_____

_____

_____

> As you review your list/answers to the questions above, look back at your joy list/legacy statement. Is there anything you would add to the list to incorporate those items into your life more?

_____

_____

_____

_____

> Look at your ideal life description. Is there anything you would add to the list to incorporate that aspiration into your life more?

_____

_____

_____

_____

> Anything else to add?

_____

_____

_____

_____

Looking at your list, answer the following:

> What are some things you could do right now, or are willing to do right now, to give yourself a raise in Soul Salary? (Highlight or mark them green.)
> What are some things you could do this month? (Highlight or mark them pink.)
> What are some things you could do this year? (Highlight or mark them orange.)
> What are some things you could do in the next five years?(Highlight or mark them blue.)

Raise S.M.A.R.T. Goal Exercise:

Let's make an intentional decision to do one of the things to raise your Soul Salary today. Set your first goal below:

> What is one thing you will do first to raise your Soul Salary? Use the S.M.A.R.T (specific, measurable, achievable, relevant, timely) goal framework:

   ✦ Specific goal:

   _____

   _____

   _____

✦ How will it be Measured (how will you
   know you have been successful):

   _____

   _____

✦ Is this goal Achievable (if not, break it into
   smaller steps) and how:

   _____

   _____

   _____

   _____

✦ Is this goal Relevant to increasing your Soul
   Salary paychecks by raising your joy (joy
   list), fulfillment (legacy statement) and/or
   basic needs and nonnegotiables?

   _____

   _____

✦ When will you reach this goal? Make it Timely:

   _____

   _____

❯ What help do you need to make this happen? How are
   you going to make space for this change in your life?

   _____

   _____

   _____

   _____

   _____

CHAPTER 8

Time for a Promotion

Promotions Exercise

Answer these open-ended questions to see where you are at right now:

> What is your Soul Salary worth to you?

_____

_____

_____

> How far are you willing to go to raise your Soul Salary and become a High Earner?

_____

_____

_____

> Pick one idea for a promotion and write the pros and cons.

  ✦ Promotion:

  _____

  _____

  _____

  _____

  ✦ Benefits:

  _____

  _____

  _____

  _____

  ✦ Risks:

  _____

  _____

  _____

  _____

> What are some actions you can take to eliminate or mitigate the risks?

  _____

  _____

  _____

  _____

  _____

  _____

Step 3
Soul Salary Bills

CHAPTER 9

Joy Killers

Joy Killers Exercise:

Let's identify some of the expectations you carry for yourself or from others. By doing so, we can become aware of what is driving you, then identify which expectations feel authentic to you and who you want to be.

> Start by noticing expectations you have for yourself. Make a (nonjudgmental) list below:

_____

_____

_____

_____

_____

_____

_____

_____

> ➤ Now let's notice expectations others have for you (e.g., significant other, parents, kids, work, etc.):

_____

_____

_____

_____

_____

_____

_____

_____

_____

_____

Review this list. Put a star next to expectations that feel authentic to you and an X next to expectations that do not feel authentic to you.

CHAPTER 10

Soul Suckers

Soul Suckers Exercise:

Create your Soul Sucker List by defining the obstacles between you and your fulfillment and legacy.

> What is causing the gap from where you are today to meeting your legacy statement from Chapter 5?

_____

_____

_____

_____

_____

> What is getting in your way and stopping you from feeling fulfilled?

_____

_____

_____

_____

_____

➤ What are your fears? (See list of common fear triggers in Chapter 10.)

_____

_____

_____

_____

_____

_____

_____

_____

_____

➤ What are your limiting beliefs? (See list of common ones in Chapter 10.)

_____

_____

_____

_____

_____

_____

_____

_____

_____

> What are you *not* proud of?

_____

_____

_____

_____

Compare this list with your Joy Killers list, and any common themes between the two are your biggest Soul Salary bills.

_____

_____

_____

_____

_____

_____

_____

Step 4
Budgeting and Budget Cuts

CHAPTER 11

Toodles, Joy Killers

Expectations and Boundary Editing Exercise:

Edit the expectations you listed in the Joy Killer chapter to be only ones that feel authentic and aligned with who you want to be. Reframe them here to be healthy self-expectations.

_____

_____

_____

_____

_____

_____

_____

_____

_____

_____

Where do you need to add boundaries to expectations others have of you or your own out-of-touch expectations?

_____

_____

_____

_____

_____

_____

Intention Exercise:

What is your intention for today?

_____

_____

What are your top three critical tasks for today?

1. Priority #1

   _____

   _____

2. Priority #2

   _____

   _____

3. Priority #3

   _____

   _____

Do they align with your intention? If not, how can you alter them to align?

_____

_____

What is your intention for the week?

_____

_____

What are your top three critical tasks for this week?

1.   Priority #1

_____

_____

2.   Priority #2

_____

_____

3.   Priority #3

_____

_____

Do they align with your intention? If not, how can you alter them to align?

_____

_____

_____

Reflections?

_____

_____

_____

_____

How did the exercise feel?

_____

_____

_____

_____

_____

_____

_____

✦ ✦ ✦ ✦ ✦

CHAPTER 12

So Long, Soul Suckers

> Journal your fears: Review the fears you wrote in Chapter 10 and empty out all of the thoughts related to those fears. Write it all out—yes, everything! Don't put your pen down!

_____

_____

_____

_____

_____

_____

_____

_____

_____

_____

_____

_____

_____

_____

> Focus on what you can control.
>> ✦ Read the journaling of your fears and cross out what you _cannot_ control.
>> ✦ Read through what you just crossed out. I suggest closing your eyes and taking three deep breaths. As you exhale, loudly and aggressively sigh out your breath as you physically let go of those items you cannot control.
> Make action plans for what you _can_ control.
>> ✦ Read the remaining fears and rank them from first to last in terms of power the fear has over you right now.
>> ✦ Use this list to write out actions you could take to mitigate them, support yourself through them, and/or eliminate each fear for the top three fears.

Fear 1

_____

_____

_____

_____

_____

Fear 2

_____

_____

_____

_____

_____

Fear 3

_____

_____

_____

_____

_____

> Prioritize.
>   + Read this list of actions and number each one
>   1, 2, or 3 based on how big of an impact that
>   action would have on addressing your fear, 1
>   being a big impact and 3 being a small impact.

> Do it!
>   + Take action starting with the big-impact items
>   ranked 1 and working down the list. Each step
>   you take brings you closer and closer to joy
>   and fulfillment.

_____

_____

_____

_____

Redefining Limiting Beliefs Exercise:

Do this with at least the top five limiting beliefs from the Chapter 10 exercise that feel the most restrictive to you today. Make sure the redefined belief feels authentic and believable to you.

Old belief:

_____

_____

New redefined belief:

_____

_____

Old belief:

_____

_____

New redefined belief:

_____

_____

Old belief:

_____

_____

New redefined belief:

_____

_____

Old belief:

_____

_____

New redefined belief:

_____

_____

Old belief:

_____

_____

New redefined belief:

_____

_____

Affirmations Exercise:

Write out some affirmations that make you feel positive and uplifted. Write them as if they are already true.

_____

_____

_____

_____

_____

_____

CHAPTER 13

Budget Cuts

Pick one Joy Killer and one Soul Sucker to do budget cuts on from your lists in Chapters 9 and 10, then write out four options for each.

Joy Killer:

_____

_____

Eliminate:

_____

_____

Delegate:

_____

_____

Reduce:

_____

_____

Add fun to:

_____

_____

Soul Sucker:

_____

_____

Eliminate:

_____

_____

Delegate:

_____

_____

Reduce:

_____

_____

Add fun to:

_____

_____

Budgeting S.M.A.R.T. Goal Exercise:

Set your first goal below:

> What is one thing you will do first to reduce your bills? Use the S.M.A.R.T (specific, measurable, achievable, relevant, timely) goal framework:
>
> ✦ Specific goal:

_____

_____

_____

_____

✦ How will it be Measured (how will you know you have been successful):

_____

_____

✦ Is this goal Achievable (if not, break it into smaller steps) and how:

_____

_____

_____

_____

✦ Is this goal Relevant to reducing your Soul Salary bills by letting go of Joy Killers and Soul Suckers?

_____

_____

_____

✦ When will you reach this goal? Make it Timely:

_____

_____

➤ What help do you need to make this happen?
  ✦ Examples: Learning material (a book, course, teacher), support from others (family member, travel agent, therapist), time (vacation time, time without kids), money.

_____

_____

_____

_____

  ✦ Don't forget your nonnegotiables (i.e., boundaries) and the conversations or steps that need to happen here.

_____

_____

_____

_____

✦ ✦ ✦ ✦ ✦

Acknowledgments

I want to acknowledge my supportive soulmate and partner in life, Henry, and my kind, passionate, and joyful kiddos, Riley and Parker. I hope this book reminds my kids to always be themselves.

And to my fur babies, our cats Simba and Clifford, for all the lap snuggles and sitting on my keyboard when I am trying to work.

As I say in the book: Allow others to have a role in your life. Your true soul tribe is eager to support you and is honored you want them as part of your squad. So here's to my soul tribe: Mom and Dad (Cathy and Stuart), Mila and Oleg, Lindsey and Jake, extended family (especially my cousins), dear friends, loving neighbors, supportive readers, and my physical, mental, and energy-wellness team.

I extend my sincere thanks to my Beta Readers (Rachel, Henry, Brittney, Sabrina, Lauren, Lindsey, Kori), my Launch team (you know who you are!), Self Publishing School and my editors (the team at Wandering Words Media).

Want More?

Check out my website to engage in my other services, such as speaking, life coaching, digital courses, and beyond!

www.JessKaskov.com

✦ ✦ ✦ ✦ ✦

Author Bio

Jessica Kaskov is an author, speaker, life coach, and thought leader who inspires the world to profound joy and fulfillment. She left her successful, fifteen-year engineering career at a Fortune 500 company to start her own business (Joyfulness with Jess), trading her hard hats for headbands. Today, she does what she feels called to do—motivating and supporting others. She lives in the suburbs of Chicago with her encouraging husband, two active sons, and two lazy cats.

Please Write a Review!

Thank You For Reading My Book!

I really appreciate all of your feedback, and
I love hearing what you have to say.

Please take two minutes now to leave a helpful review on
Amazon letting me know what you thought of the book:
www.JessKaskov.com/review

Thank you so much!
Warmly,
Jess